Britten

Christopher Headington

The Illustrated Lives of the Great Composers.

Britten

Christopher Headington

OMNIBUS PRESS
LONDON · NEW YORK · SYDNEY

To Roy Westbrook, friend and fellow Britten enthusiast, and his family.

Cover design and art direction by Pearce Marchbank.
Cover photography by Julian Hawkins
Text design, scanning and film origination by Hilite

Copyright © 1996 by Christopher Headington
This edition published in 1996 by Omnibus Press, a division of Book Sales Limited

ISBN 0.7117.4812.7
Order No. OP47746

Exclusive Distributors
Book Sales Limited,
8/9 Frith Street,
London W1V 5TZ, UK.

Music Sales Corporation,
257 Park Avenue South,
New York, NY 10010, USA.

Music Sales Pty Limited,
120 Rothschild Avenue,
Rosebery, NSW 2018, Australia.

To the Music Trade only:
Music Sales Limited,
8/9 Frith Street,
London W1V 5TZ, UK.

Printed in the United Kingdom by Staples Printers Limited, Rochester, Kent.

A catalogue record for this book is available from the British Library.

Contents

1   The Boy and his Background   1

2   The Young Professional   14

3   America   27

4   Wartime England and *Peter Grimes*   40

5   Sussex and Suffolk   54

6   Salvation at Sea   72

7   West meets East   87

8   With Aschenbach in Venice   107

9   'A time there was...'   123

     Catalogue of works   133

     Bibliography   137

     Discography   139

     Further Reference   141

     Index   147

Chapter 1

The Boy and his Background

The engagement photograph of Robert Victor Britten and Edith Rhoda Hockey, circa 1900.

'I come from a very ordinary middle-class family', said Benjamin Britten in 1968. 40 years before that, his mother had claimed that this was the first time a musical genius had come from the middle classes, rather than the lower classes or aristocracy – though that was hardly true. His father's position as a respected Lowestoft dentist was in that middle ground of society, far above the town's fisherfolk and shopkeepers yet not one of the county set of the local yacht club. Nevertheless, Robert Britten could afford to employ a household servant and a nanny for his four children, and could send those children to private schools. The fourth, an unplanned late arrival, was christened Edward Benjamin, the latter name being after that of Jacob's youngest son in the Biblical story. The first of these names was soon dropped in favour of the second, usually shortened to 'Beni'.

He was born on 22 November 1913, the feast day of music's patron saint, St Cecilia. Long afterwards, he told his publisher Donald Mitchell that he could remember his birth and 'the sound of rushing water', but to someone else he said that his first memory was of hearing the explosion of a German bomb. His sister Beth declared that once, when lying in his perambulator in the garden, he woke up crying and said 'Bomb drop on Dear's head'. 'Dear' became his name for himself, she said, because he heard it so often from people exclaiming in delight at his blue eyes, fair curls and rosy cheeks: 'he was a very, very fetching little boy'. According to his other sister, Barbara, their mother Edith adored him: 'he was always allowed to do everything...he was her baby, and everything he did was always perfect'. Doubtless this was partly because he was considered delicate, having been left with a heart murmur by infantile pneumonia. On the other hand, his father, known as 'Pop', was relatively strict, and the children had to stand up when he came into the room. Benjamin's brother Robert (Bobby), later a headmaster, said, 'We were a bit afraid of our father.'

The Britten family's house at 21 Kirkley Cliff Road in Lowestoft.

Edith Rhoda Britten, probably in her early twenties.

The family's house in Kirkley Cliff Road was large and comfortable, with good furniture, a piano, pictures and a biggish nursery. One girl cousin later remembered it as peaceful and happy, with a party atmosphere, though another friend noted that this mood would be deliberately created for guests, and that after Bobby started taking piano lessons, he would quickly be told, 'do go and play something'. Though there was no gramophone or radio, there was plenty of music, for Edith Britten had a pleasant mezzo-soprano voice, belonged to Lowestoft's music society and often entertained visiting professional singers. Sometimes she performed as a soloist at local concerts, which usually took place in St John's, a church of evangelical persuasion where she and her children (though not her husband) worshipped every Sunday.

Benjamin's first musical memory was of his mother singing, and, in 1968, he was to say that, for him, musical perfection lay in 'the human voice singing beautifully...one's mother...trying to make one go to sleep when one's two years old' (he was a poor sleeper). She was the dominant, adored figure of his childhood, to whom, at the age of nine, he signed a letter, 'Your own tiny little (sick-for-Muvver) BENI'. As a teenager he still referred to her in his diary as 'my darling'. Her influence went deep, and not only on a personal level: it may even have shaped his professional career, for according to Freud, 'if a man has been his mother's undisputed darling he retains throughout life the triumphant feeling, the confidence in success, which not seldom brings actual success'. A boyhood friend, Basil Reeve, recalled Mrs Britten saying that music's famous 'three B's' – Bach, Beethoven and Brahms – should have their successor in Britten and that she 'was determined that he should be a great musician'. In this sense, he thought her 'formidable', although she was generally liked.

But her favourite son's interests were not only musical. At three, Benjamin dressed as an elf for a family production of *Cinderella*, and at five he played Tom in a stage version of Kingsley's *The Water Babies*, as he later recalled, 'in skin-coloured tights, with madly curly hair'. A year later, he wrote a five-page miniature play of his own called *The Royal Falily* (sic)[1] which contains a snatch of music, just four bars which fail to make real sense. He also liked trains, and Beth remembered him lying in the bath reading a rail timetable.

Dressed as an elf, Britten sits second from the left in the front row. His sister Barbara stands on the far left of the back row, his brother Robert stands third from the left and his sister Beth kneels on one knee in front of Robert.

Benjamin Britten, sitting on his mother's knee, poses with other members of a cast of *The Water Babies*.

At seven, he began proper piano lessons with a young local teacher, Ethel Astle, and, before long, he could accompany his mother's singing and join her, or the local organist Charles Coleman, in piano duets. Soon he attempted composition: one early sketch 'looked rather like the Forth Bridge, hundreds of dots all over the page connected by long lines...I am afraid it was the pattern on the paper which I was interested in', and he was much upset when his mother said it was unplayable. Undeterred, he would improvise pianistic tone poems inspired by domestic events or other local matters. One such was a shipwreck, for the Britten house actually faced the North Sea and, from his earliest days, he knew its changing moods and alarming power.

Otherwise this child's home life was one of ordinary things like bike rides, bracing swims in the sea, fêtes and country fairs, storybooks, toys and games indoors and out, and playing with the family dog Caesar. Family 'snaps' represent his time and place: the four-year-old in white socks sitting on a leopard-skin rug and playing with a toy ship, the lad of seven outdoors with rumpled socks, short trousers over bony knees and holding anxiously on to a floppy hat. A picture taken on the lawn shows a summer tea party with the adults at table and the children on the grass: the tea things, lace tablecloth, parasol, deck and basket chairs, white dresses and cricket flannels all speak of an England long past, a time when the British Empire was a major force and much of the world map coloured red.

At eight, Benjamin went as a day boy to a nearby preparatory school called South Lodge. He had seemingly left his health troubles behind and was energetic and, he said later, '...quite an ordinary little boy [who] loved cricket...adored mathematics...behaved fairly well, only ragged the recognised amount, so that his contacts with the cane or the slipper were happily rare (although one nocturnal expedition to stalk ghosts left its marks behind)'. Yet he was not really so ordinary: even at the time, he voiced his shock at the 'slipperings' and canings which were everyday school

South Lodge, the preparatory school Britten attended as a day boy.

4

Britten, aged 10 or 11.

occurrences, and later he was to wonder whether his pacifist beliefs had their roots in this early reaction against violence. Towards the end of his time at South Lodge, he wrote an anti-hunting, pacifist essay which was not well received by his teachers. But he did well at lessons, athletics and cricket, becoming head boy just before his fourteenth birthday.

Of course, the most unusual thing about this schoolboy was that he now wrote a great deal of music. At nine, he bound up some of his songs into a volume for his parents, and his piano compositions included sonatas, suites and 'waltztes' (sic)[1]. Over 40 years later he revised and published five of the latter written between 1923-25. He wrote string quartets and other chamber pieces, including, in his thirteenth year, two for violin, cello and piano called 'trios in fantastic form', and by the age of fourteen, there were also a *Symphony in D minor* and an ambitious *'Symphonic Poem in E'* called *Chaos and Cosmos*, of which he later remarked ruefully that he 'was not sure what those terms really meant'.

Though young E. B. Britten was no keyboard prodigy, his piano playing also progressed. He passed his Associated Board Grade 5 exam at ten and Grade 8 (Final) at twelve. At ten, he also began viola lessons with Audrey Alston, a clergyman's wife living not far away in Framlingham Earl, who also encouraged him to attend concerts. Thus, in October 1924, he heard the English composer Frank Bridge conduct his orchestral suite *The Sea* at the Norwich Festival and was, in his own words, 'knocked sideways', not least by its colourful sound. So far, he had had little contact with modern music, but he had been excited by what reached him, including Holst's *The Planets* and Ravel's *String Quartet*. Now Bridge's music seemed to open new doors.

Frank Bridge, who took Britten on as a composition pupil in 1927.

As a budding composer, Benjamin clearly needed professional guidance, but no such guidance was available locally. However, when Frank Bridge returned to Norwich in 1927 with another new work called *Enter Spring*, Mrs Alston introduced her pupil to him. Bridge asked to see some of his music and liked what he saw, which included a 91-page orchestral *Overture in B flat minor*. He then agreed to take him on as a composition pupil – surprisingly, for he had no others – and also recommended that the boy should receive piano lessons from his colleague Harold Samuel. After some hesitation, Robert and Edith Britten agreed that he should make day-trips to London for this purpose.

In his diary, Benjamin called his first composition lesson with Bridge, which took place on 12 January 1928, 'absolutely wonderful'. But this teacher was strict and demanding, and sessions could be over two hours in length: 'often I used to end these marathons in tears; not that he was beastly to me, but the concentrated strain was too much for me'. He also realised how much he still had to learn:

'I, who thought I was already on the verge of immortality, saw my illusions shattered...I felt I was very small fry.'

Later he said, 'It was just the right treatment for me', but in the meantime he wrote less and thought more.

The young composer's music gained individuality as his personality developed. Though an orchestral piece of March 1928 called *Humoureske* (sic) is gauche in character, its instrumentation (a subject he had not yet studied) is surprisingly effective. The same is true of the *Quatre Chansons Françaises*, remarkably imaginative settings of Hugo and Verlaine dating from the summer of the same year: here there is shape, imagination and sensitivity, although we can probably detect the influence of Ravel's cycle *Shéhérazade* in the subtle word-setting and sensuously delicate orchestral sound. We may also suspect the influence of the Austrian composer Alban Berg, whom Bridge admired; furthermore, Berg and Ravel had the common background of Wagner, then among the young composer's heroes. But most surprising of all in these French songs is this schoolboy's choice of disillusioned *fin de siècle* poems and his music's consequent bitter world-weariness. One perspicacious Britten expert, the late Christopher Palmer, judged it remarkable that already in this early work the composer demonstrated his lifelong preoccupation with 'the vulnerability of innocence'.

Poets, too, had written of innocence and experience: William Blake saw these two conditions as successive, with brightness giving way to gloom, while Wordsworth wrote of the 'shades of the prison-house' that gradually encircle a growing mind. With adolescence, the hitherto outgoing young Britten changed and became shy and moody, and his sexuality seems to have been involved. A woman friend, Beata Sauerlander, who nursed him through a high fever in 1940, remembers:

...he did talk about his schooldays, about his childhood. And although I can't remember exactly what he said, I remember that he had very traumatic experiences, sexual experiences. And it bothered him.

One more piece of evidence for this exists. According to Britten's collaborator Eric Crozier, the composer told him that he was 'raped' by a master at his school. But Crozier, who died in 1994, divulged this only after Britten's death and his remains the only testimony relating to this. If it truly happened, it is impossible to believe that Britten never told his lifelong companion, the singer Peter Pears. Nearly three years his senior, Pears outlived Britten by ten years, yet never mentioned it and indeed called his childhood 'idyllic'. Though sexuality is clearly relevant to Britten's somewhat uneasy adult personality and to his lifestyle having become homosexual at a time when this was a criminal offence in Britain, we should also remember more positively that his 35-year partnership with Pears (a marriage in all but name) was both happy and artistically so fruitful that it helped him to win his country's highest honours.

Gresham's School in Holt, Norfolk, where Britten spent two uneasy years.

In September 1928, Britten went on to his public school, Gresham's School, at Holt in Norfolk. Almost the first person he met was the music master, Walter Greatorex, who greeted him sarcastically with the words, 'So *you* are the little boy who likes Stravinsky!' and, perhaps resenting his lessons in London, soon criticised his piano technique. 'He as good as said I had none at all', the boy miserably reported in a letter home, adding that he was no longer allowed to play the Beethoven pieces that he liked and had been told he had no hope of entering the musical profession: 'Music in this school is now finished for me!' – though he fought back, calling his teacher's own playing uncoordinated and harsh.

Undoubtedly Gresham's School came as a shock to this sensitive boy. He hated the swearing and vulgarity of the three others with whom he shared a study, and comforted himself by reading Bible texts important to him since his recent confirmation, writing in his diary, 'My duty towards God is to believe in him, to fear him, and to love him, with all my heart'. He was once tossed in a blanket and then into water; but, as he told his sister Beth (though keeping the incident from his mother), this made him faint, which scared his tormentors and caused them thereafter to leave him alone. Later he hoped to organise 'an effort against Bullying', but it seems to have come to nothing. His tension was sometimes reflected in illness, mostly sore throats, and he was at least once seriously unhappy, writing in January 1930:

'How I loathe this abominable hole...I simply cannot see how I can bare (sic) up through it, & suicide is so cowardly. Running away's as bad; so I suppose I've got to stick it.'

Peter Pears was later to write of Britten's 'two uneasy years' at Gresham's, and this unease affected the composer's memories of school music, for he later wrote bitterly, 'At my public school my musical education was practically non-existent', and that originality was 'completely discouraged'. Yet the facts are not so simple. He liked singing alto in the chapel choir and hearing Stravinsky's ballet *The Firebird* on the school gramophone, and his violin-playing housemaster sometimes invited him to his study to listen to radio concerts: one was 'a marvellous Schönberg concert' including *Pierrot lunaire*[2]. There were chamber concerts at which he played the viola, earning praise in the school magazine for December 1929 as 'a very reliable musician'; the *Gresham* also admired him as a pianist who showed 'just the right delicacy of touch and quiet feeling' in a Chopin nocturne and waltz. In the following term, Walter Greatorex joined Britten (playing viola) and the string teacher Joyce Chapman in a performance of the young composer's *Bagatelle* for violin, viola and piano. 'Written in a modern idiom, the Trio shows that Britten has already advanced a considerable distance in the technique of composition', the *Gresham* opined pompously: 'He should go far...' Later in 1930, the school chaplain wrote with less reserve, declaring that this pupil was the finest musician ever to have attended the school: 'the *Polichinelle* of Rachmaninoff held one bewildered, spellbound...of course Britten was encored.' The encore was a Brahms waltz.

Before entering Gresham's, Britten had extracted a promise from his parents that upon obtaining his School Certificate there he could leave and begin full-time musical training in London. But in May 1930 he noted delightedly in his diary that 'Pop' had said that he would leave at the end of this summer term, whatever happened. With his parents' approval, he entered for a composition scholarship at the Royal College of Music, submitting the necessary examples of his work, and was then summoned on 19 June for written papers and an interview with the examiners Ralph Vaughan Williams, John Ireland and Sidney Waddington. He was given the result at once, and wrote in his diary that evening, 'I have surprise of winning'. 'Congratulations!', wrote Frank Bridge. Next, as a bonus, he passed School Certificate with five credits and his headmaster was 'delighted...he is such a dear boy and so modest about all his brilliant performances'. He left Gresham's with various prizes, choosing books and scores ranging from *Pierrot lunaire* to *The Oxford Book of English Verse*, and, despite his passionate wish to press on with his music, now regretted leaving some of his school friends, 'such boys as these...I didn't think I should be so sorry to leave'.

Barbara Britten in the 1920s.

Britten started at the Royal College in the autumn of 1930, lodging in nearby Bayswater under the caring eye of his sister Barbara, who also lived in London. His piano teacher was Arthur Benjamin, a cheerful Australian in his forties whom he liked, but it was not long before he was told that he was 'not

The Royal College of Music, London, photographed in the 1930s.

built for a solo pianist – how I am going to make my pennies Heaven only knows', and admitted as much to himself: 'Lor', I'm bad at the piano!'. His composition teacher, recommended by Frank Bridge, was John Ireland, a composer of individuality and some importance. But here there were other problems: he found Ireland dishearteningly critical and especially disliked going to his untidy Chelsea house for lessons; later he confided to a friend that this glum bachelor once made a sexual pass at him. Long afterwards, in 1954, Ireland said that Britten's lessons with Bridge had not constituted a real course of study and that he had therefore needed 'a good deal of time over counterpoint, fugue & allied subjects', but that he was also the finest College musician in generations. Britten, in turn, was later to say, and probably with justice, that Ireland nursed him 'very gently through a very, very difficult musical adolescence', and, whatever the friction between them, the student did his best to respond to his teacher's guidance. In his diary for 8 May 1931 Britten noted with satisfaction that Ireland was 'quite pleased' with his *Three Fugues for Piano*, written as an exercise.

In the meantime, the young student continued to see Frank Bridge and his wife Ethel, who had become valued friends, and would visit their cottage near Eastbourne to play tennis and make car trips to lovely old churches in 'tucked-away little villages' which opened his eyes to 'the magnificence of English ecclesiastical architecture'. The older man, who had written a piano sonata in memory of a friend killed in the First World War, also introduced him to the concept of pacifism.

Although Bridge now properly refrained from teaching Britten music, he continued to influence his development and taste. Beethoven and Brahms, the musical idols of his boyhood, remained so (he had a picture of Brahms in his London bedsit and a bust of Beethoven at home), but, as his diary tells us, he also followed everything that was new in music and went to hear Stravinsky and Schönberg perform their own works in London concerts. He wrote of *Le sacre du printemps* in January 1931: 'bewildering and terrifying; I didn't really enjoy it, but I think it's incredibly marvellous and arresting', and, by September 1932, it was 'the World's Wonder'. As for Schönberg, 'Heaven only knows!!'. He also discovered a passion for Mahler at a time when that composer's music was little known in Britain and not much admired (Vaughan Williams called him 'a very tolerable imitation of a composer'). Much British music – 'English', as people said then – repelled him as reflecting an 'amateurish and folksy' attitude that he also disliked at the Royal College of Music. '1 min of Elgar Symphony 2 but can stand no more', he wrote of a broadcast, and 'Didn't like Bax – bored with it' is another typical comment. Although he enjoyed singing in Vaughan Williams's *Fantasia on Christmas Carols*, later he was to say that he made 'a struggle away from everything Vaughan Williams seemed to stand for', although Delius's *Brigg Fair* appealed. Among younger composers, William Walton, 11 years his senior, impressed him with *Façade* and the *Viola Concerto* – 'a work of genius'. But, loyally, he still named Frank Bridge – who did not enjoy the standing of Vaughan Williams and Ireland – as 'England's premier composer'.

Concerning his own development, he never forgot Bridge's advice: to find himself and be true to himself, saying clearly what he had to say. It was a far slower process than he had once imagined, and in the meantime he took on board a mass of musical study and experience. Inevitably, he formed strong views and prejudices, but later said that creative artists cannot avoid this. In any case, prejudice went both ways, as did tolerance. When Britten won the annual Farrar Composition Prize in July 1931, Vaughan Williams, who was one of the adjudicators, called his work 'very clever but beastly'; yet soon afterwards he recommended Britten's setting of Psalm 150 to the director of the Three Choirs Festival as 'rather good...Of course it wd never have been written except for the *Symphonie de Psaumes* [by Stravinsky] but is no worse for that'. Vaughan Williams also mentioned Britten to another concert organiser, Anne Macnaghten, saying, 'his orchestral & choral things are fine'.

Beth Britten in the 1930s.

In Britten's second year at the Royal College, he moved into different lodgings and installed a piano so that he and his student friends could play chamber music. Nevertheless, family ties remained strong: his sister Beth joined him in this house and he returned to Lowestoft as often as he could, writing that there was 'no place like home, for all the Londons in the world'. In every sphere except music, the tastes of this 18-year-old remained juvenile: he liked sweets and school stories, and was enthralled by J.M. Barrie's *Peter Pan*. With little interest in girls, he hated the Lowestoft dances that he sometimes had to attend ('much against my will & principles') and thought his brother Bobby, now engaged, 'positively unhealthy' in his affectionate behaviour towards his fiancée. In the cinema, he preferred Walt Disney's cartoons to romantic films. Emotionally, he felt safest in music, and perhaps in the company of the mother who had introduced him to music. At this time, his friend Paul Wright found him sometimes disapproving and even 'formidable' – the same word once used of his mother.

In May 1932, Britten won the Royal College of Music's Cobbett Prize for a *Phantasy* for string quintet and heard a student performance of it that he called 'bad – but I expected worse'. He also gained a Sullivan Prize amounting to £10. However, when he entered for the prestigious Mendelssohn Scholarship worth £150, the judges placed him second and awarded him £50 – still a very decent sum in those days. He was now beginning to make a name outside the College, and in 1932 the Oxford University Press published his *Three Two-part Songs* to poems by Walter de la Mare, in due course sending him a first royalty cheque for 15 shillings. On 12 December 1932, the Macnaghten-Lemare Concerts put on a performance of his *Phantasy* (which dissatisfied him) and the newly published *Two-Part Songs*. However, John Ireland, having taken the trouble to be present, said no word to the composer. Furthermore, the critic Christian Darnton in the journal *Music Lover* called the string work technically inadequate and dismissed the songs as 'reminiscent in a quite peculiar degree of Walton's latest songs'. Years later, Britten still remembered and resented this comment, writing in the journal *Opera* for February 1952:

'Now anyone who is interested can see for himself that this is silly nonsense...It is easy to imagine the damping effect of this first notice on a young composer. I was furious and dismayed because I could see there was not a word of truth in it. I was also considerably discouraged. No friendliness – no encouragement – no perception. Was this the critical treatment which one was to expect all one's life? A gloomy outlook.'

Britten once said, 'I never read the critics, praise or blame' – though this was not strictly true. It was typical of him to smart under adverse criticism but seemingly shrug off praise, so that we do not know how he felt when, soon afterwards, another new work of his impressed the same critic, Darnton. When on 31 January 1933, the Macnaghten-Lemare Concerts gave the première of his Sinfonietta for ten instruments (dedicated to Bridge), Darnton saluted it as 'a really outstanding work [and] a great advance...The Sinfonietta contained some exceedingly stimulating musical thought, considerable constructive power and surprising technical skill'. The *Daily Telegraph* more cautiously called the composer 'as provocative as any of the foreign exponents

MACNAGHTEN-LEMARE CONCERTS

The last concert in this enterprising series of works by young English composers consisted, with one exception, of pieces written during the past year, which were being given their first performance. The writers are for the most part working along recognizable lines, but Mr. Benjamin Britten, after taking something from Hindemith, seems to be striking out on a path of his own. His *Sinfonietta* for 10 instruments (five strings, four wood-wind, and horn), shows that he possesses a power of invention apart from the efficiency with which he handles his material. The work, which is in three movements (*Poco presto—Andante—Tarantella*) is throughout strongly rhythmical; in fact the last movement, which grows into a frenzy that completely suggests the traditional origin of the dance, is built out of rhythmic figures rather than purely musical themes. On this occasion Mr. Britten permits himself to indulge effects of barbarism, which at least hold the attention. He has already enough to say for himself to excuse his independence of tradition. Mr. Gordon Jacob's new *Serenade* for five wind instruments is a suite of short movements alternately of a meandering beauty and of bright witty dialogue between the players, including a duet for piccolo and bassoon. Mr. H. K. Andrews's *Concerto* for oboe and chamber orchestra is a lively piece of writing in a not very interesting manner. The solo part was played with beautiful smoothness by Miss Sylvia Spencer. An *Introit* for small orchestra and solo violin, by Mr. Gerald Finzi, which dates from some years ago, is written with dignity, though its main theme seemed rather shapeless. Miss Grace Williams's Movement for Trumpet and Chamber Orchestra proved too much for the small theatre of the Ballet Club, and there is insufficient contrast between the colour of the orchestration and that of the solo instrument, but in spite of some resulting confusion it has freshness and brilliance. Mr. Richard Walton played the solo part very capably. Miss Iris Lemare, who has conducted and directed these concerts, handled all these varieties of new music with skill.

An excerpt from a review in *The Times* of the premiere of Britten's Sinfonietta for ten instruments, dated February 3, 1933.

of the catch-as-catch-can style of composition', but *The Times* praised him for 'striking out on a path of his own... He has already enough to say for himself to excuse his independence of tradition'.

The BBC, as a patron of new music, had already noticed Britten and arranged a broadcast performance of his *Phantasy* for February. Henceforth it followed the young composer's development with interest, and Victor Hely-Hutchinson of its music staff invited him to a meeting on 16 June 1933 to discuss his current work. Hely-Hutchinson then stated in a departmental memorandum:

'I do wholeheartedly subscribe to the general opinion that Mr Britten is the most interesting new arrival since Walton, and I feel we should watch his work very carefully.'

[1] Britten's spelling remained unreliable throughout his life.

[2] In April 1930 Britten acquired a copy of Schoenberg's *Six Little Piano Pieces*, op. 19, and performed them at Lowestoft.

Chapter 2

The Young Professional

At the end of 1933, Britten left the Royal College of Music with a travelling scholarship of £100 to further his experience. Although he wanted to study in Vienna with Berg, his parents vetoed this plan, possibly because of College disapproval of Berg's 'advanced' style. However, in March 1934 he went to Florence and the Festival of the International Society for Contemporary Music and heard Leon Goossens and the Griller Quartet play his *Phantasy* for oboe quartet, dating (like his string *Phantasy*) from 1932, 'very beautifully & it's quite well received'.

Shortly before that, another new piece had been premièred. This was a 30-minute set of choral variations called *A Boy was Born*, which the BBC Singers broadcast on 23 February 1934. Completed the previous May, it had taken Britten six months to write, for he no longer enjoyed the compositional facility of his schooldays. He was delighted with his performers ('They sing like angels'), and even before the broadcast the BBC's journal *Radio Times* saluted the work as 'yet another sign of the growing vitality of modern English music...there is no trace of fumbling, nor, which is even more remarkable, of outside influences'. With hindsight we may see this date of 23 February 1934, which was also that of Elgar's death, as marking a turning point in British music, for a new generation of composers led by Walton was emerging, who wished to escape the heavy folk influence evident in Vaughan Williams and his followers without throwing over the past or sacrificing a certain indefinable Englishness.[1] Thus while *A Boy was Born*, as a setting of English carol texts for a choir including boys' voices, reflected a lengthy church tradition, it showed no conscious folkiness. Oddly enough, it was also in that year that Vaughan Williams shocked some people with his trenchant *Fourth Symphony*, and much later, in 1943, he was to write: 'Are we old fogeys of the Folk-song movement getting into a rut? If so, it is very good for us to be pulled out of it by such fiery young steeds as Benjamin Britten...Welcome, then, the younger generation who will push along the highway.'

Britten dedicated *A Boy was Born* to his father. Robert Britten had been ill for several months with cancer and died on 6 April while his son was in Italy. Britten hastened home for the funeral, at which part of *A Boy was Born* was performed along with the final chorus of Bach's *St Matthew Passion*. 'Mum is a perfect marvel...bearing up incredibly', he wrote. She had been left very comfortably off with about £15,000, and while her children received only £100 each in the will, they too were to benefit substantially when she herself died three years later. In any case, all save Benjamin were now self-supporting. After the funeral, the young composer took his mother to Robert Britten's prep school in Wales to recuperate. For the boys of this school he wrote a set of 12 songs with piano called *Friday Afternoons,* the title reflecting the time of their singing practices. They are lively and sometimes jazzy pieces, full of energy and wit, and sensibly make no excessive demands on untrained young voices, whereas *A Boy was Born,* intended for professionals, is taxing both vocally and interpretatively.

Although the Oxford University Press had taken Britten's *A Boy was Born* and a *Simple Symphony* for strings based on boyhood

Ralph Hawkes of Boosey & Hawkes, who became Britten's regular publishers in the early 1930s.

15

pieces, they had not yet accepted his *Sinfonietta*, and when they turned down his *Phantasy* for oboe quartet as uncommercial he approached another firm, Boosey & Hawkes, who now became his regular publishers. Ralph Hawkes accepted the *Sinfonietta* and *Friday Afternoons*, and commissioned a piano suite called *Holiday Diary* which Britten called 'impressions of a boy's seaside holiday, in pre-war days': its movement titles, such as 'Early morning bathe' and 'Funfair', again remind us of his nostalgia for childhood. But he had difficulty in writing 'these hellish pft pieces' dedicated to Arthur Benjamin: his relationship with the piano was to remain uneasy and he wrote little solo music for the instrument although he played it with skill and subtlety. *Holiday Diary* had its première in London on 30 November 1934, given by Betty Humby (who later married the conductor Sir Thomas Beecham).

In October 1934, Britten went abroad again, this time with his mother, using his College grant to tour Europe and perhaps meet influential musicians. In Basle, Salzburg, Vienna, Munich and finally Paris they attended concerts and operas: Vienna particularly thrilled him by three Wagner performances including one of *Die Meistersinger* on 13 November ('incredible vitality, modernity, richness in lovely melody, humour, pathos in fact every favourable quality'), though he was sorry that Berg was not in the city. As for Mrs Britten, now in her sixties, she had occasional dizzy spells and had to be looked after; inevitably, this mother and son were less close than in his boyhood, and he could not subscribe to her belief that she was now receiving psychic messages from her husband. She, too, can have had little sympathy for the central-European brittleness of the *Suite for violin and piano* which he was now writing.

Back in England, Britten had to think about a job, and he applied to the BBC, though with reluctance at the thought of administrative work. But then, in April 1935, a phone call inviting him to contact the film director Alberto Cavalcanti led to a lunch with Cavalcanti and his fellow director William Coldstream and an invitation to compose music for a film made by the GPO (Post Office) film unit. Britten readily accepted and showed such aptitude that this soon led to a more permanent arrangement. Between 1935 and 1939 he was to compose scores for nearly twenty small-budget documentary films and thus gain immensely valuable practical experience. He was to say in 1946, in a BBC broadcast talk called *The Composer and the Listener:*

'I had to work quickly, to force myself to work when I didn't want to, and to get used to working in all kinds of circumstances...I had to write scores for not more than six or seven players, and to make those instruments make all the effects that each film demanded...I well remember the mess we made in the studio one day when trying to fit an appropriate sound to shots of a large ship unloading in a dock. We had pails of water which we slopped everywhere, drain-pipes with coal slipping down them, whistles and every kind of paraphernalia we could think of.'

A still from the film *Night Mail*.

Britten's film work, which also led to work in the theatre, brought him into contact with an exceptionally gifted man who was to become a close friend, the poet Wystan Auden. In the films *Coal Face* and *Night Mail*, he collaborated with Auden, who was nearly seven years older than he and had already made his reputation. Auden had also been at Gresham's School and then gone on to Christ Church, Oxford; his first book of poems had appeared in 1930 and his work now reflected Marxist and psychoanalytical ideas. Later, Britten was to call Auden 'a powerful, revolutionary person. He was very much anti-bourgeois and that appealed'. Auden, in his turn, quickly recognised Britten's extraordinary musical sensitivity in relation to the English language, but decided he needed bringing out of his provincial shell.

Wystan Auden, right, and
Christopher Isherwood
photographed in 1938.

Auden's influence helped to make Britten more of a political
activist. By 1935, he felt strongly enough about pacifism to
distribute leaflets in Lowestoft – 'a foul job, but it may make
people use their brains', and argue with 'die-hards – Indian
Colonels, army widows, typical old spinsters etc!'. He told Marjorie
Fass approvingly of Auden's view that all artists must oppose
Fascism, 'which of course restricts all freedom of thought', and in
1936 he composed music for the pacifist film *Peace of Britain.* We
know from his diaries that he deplored Mussolini's conquest of
Abyssinia (now Ethiopia) and what he considered to be the
feeble response of other nations to such aggression. It is hard
to say how much of this was directly due to Auden, but their
growing friendship eased his development into a more
independent, left-wing and cosmopolitan person. His growing
political awareness even affected his views on music, and he
wrote of Elgar's 'First Symphony' in his diary for 5 September
1935 that 'only in Imperialistic England could such a work be
tolerated.'

Britten was now travelling more, and further, and in April
1936 he went by air to the ISCM Festival in Barcelona to
partner Antonio Brosa in the première of his *Suite for violin and
piano.* While there, he heard the premiere of Berg's *Violin
Concerto,* which he found 'just shattering – very simple, &
touching' (Berg had recently died), and made new English

18

The composer Lennox Berkeley in 1936.

friends in the young writer Peter Burra and the composer Lennox Berkeley, whose music was also being performed. A year later, he and Berkeley were to compose two movements each of an orchestral suite of Catalan dance tunes and call it *Mont Juic* after a Barcelona park.

Returning to England, Britten now worked with Auden on an ambitiously large concert work, a song cycle with orchestra called *Our Hunting Fathers*. Its unconventional subject was animals as pests, pets and hunted creatures; of the five poems, Auden wrote only the prologue and epilogue, for 'Rats Away!' and 'Messalina' (Nos 2 and 3) were anonymous and the penultimate 'Dance of Death' was by the 17th-century poet Thomas Ravenscroft. After finishing his score that summer, the composer was 'very proud' and later he declared, 'it's my Op. 1 alright'. Yet *Our Hunting Fathers* is disturbing music, with expressionistic virtuoso writing both for the soloist and the orchestra; Peter Pears, who later performed it, called it 'spiky, exact and not at all cosy'. This applies equally to the text, for the closing lines of Auden's epilogue – 'To hunger, work illegally, / And be anonymous' – are in fact a quotation from Lenin, while Britten's juxtaposition of the words 'German' and 'Jew' (the names of two hawks in the 'Dance of Death') cannot be coincidental. Indeed, Donald Mitchell has suggested that the cycle really concerns 'man's hunting of man himself'.

The première of *Our Hunting Fathers* took place on 25 September as part of the 1936 Norwich Festival, with the soprano Sophie Wyss and Britten himself conducting the London Philharmonic Orchestra. He lacked experience and was horrified when at rehearsal some players mocked the work ('the most catastrophic evening of my life'), but matters improved and the performance was reasonably successful, so that he could write, 'The orchestra plays better than I had dared to hope...I am *very* pleased with it & it goes down well – most of the audience being interested if bewildered'. Frank Bridge was there (as was Vaughan Williams, whose *Five Tudor Portraits* was also performed), but, as Britten later admitted, did not like the new work, partly because of the edgy instrumentation. As for his mother, she disapproved 'very thoroughly of "Rats"', he noted, significantly adding, 'but that is almost an incentive – no actual insult to her tho'.' Clearly, he was enjoying his new-found independence and not sorry to let her see it. Even so, family ties remained strong, and in November he and Beth started sharing a London flat in the Finchley Road, over the shop where she worked as a dressmaker.

19

Edith Britten photographed towards the end of her life.

Britten as a young man in his twenties.

In any case, they were soon to lose their mother. In January 1937, while visiting them in London, she went down with bronchial pneumonia, and when Beth also fell seriously ill, Britten called in his other sister Barbara and temporarily moved out to make space for her. Although a specialist examined Edith Britten and was reassuring, she died on 31 January and Britten wrote in his diary:

'Mum had a heart attack at about 7.0 & died in about ten minutes without being at all conscious or suffering – thank God. So I lose the grandest mother a person could possibly have – & I only hope she realised that I felt like it. Nothing one can do eases the terrible ache that one feels – O God Almighty

'Poor old Beth mustn't be told...God – what a day!'

For all Britten's grief, this loss was a liberation, for he was already disturbingly conscious of the chasm between his family's moral values and those of Auden's set. Auden was homosexual, as was his friend and colleague Christopher Isherwood, though they were not lovers. There was also no affair between Britten and either of these men; yet together they led him to a greater awareness and acceptance of his sexuality. He was already experiencing pressures in this direction, and in a Barcelona night club with Lennox Berkeley and Peter Burra had noted 'the sexual temptations of every kind'; Berkeley later joined him in Cornwall and admitted (as Britten put it) his 'sexual weakness for young men of my age & form'. In Paris he saw a show with 'about 20 nude females, fat, hairy, unprepossessing...appalling that such a noble thing as sex should be so degraded'; a visit to Oscar Wilde's grave pleased him more – as did Notre Dame and a performance of Beethoven's moralistic opera *Fidelio*. Soon after this, he noted that a school friend who was homosexual had suggested, 'now is the time for me to decide something about my sexual life'. He spent a weekend at Peter Burra's Berkshire cottage and found him to be 'a kindred spirit in thousands of ways (one way in particular)'. Next, Christopher Isherwood took him to a Turkish bath in London's West End and he noted 'Very pleasant sensations – completely sensuous, but very healthy. It is extraordinary to find one's resistance to anything gradually weakening. The trouble was that we spent the night there – couldn't sleep a wink on the hard beds, in the perpetual restlessness of the surroundings.'

Yet Britten seems still to have remained an observer, unwilling to express his sexuality and even less to give his love: in other words, some might say, his mother still held sway. He was under tension, and it often showed. His Sussex friend Marjorie Fass described him as 'the picture of misery & depression', and feared – as did their mutual friends the Bridges – that he was on the verge of a breakdown. She had deep reservations about Auden and his influence, commenting, 'Dear Benjy he *is* so young and *so* dazzled'. She and the Bridges were also concerned as to the artistic direction Britten now seemed to be taking; so was the critic Basil Maine, who compared his achievement in *A Boy was Born* with newer music merely 'turned out to bolster up the plays and verse of Auden' and feared that he might 'dissipate his talent in an unworthy association'.

In April 1937 came the first in a series of events which in time reconciled Britten at least partially with his nature. Peter Burra died in a light aircraft accident, and shortly after attending the funeral the composer went to Burra's cottage with their mutual friend Peter Pears, a tenor in the BBC Singers, to help sort out his papers. Their shared grief brought them closer, and Britten wrote in his diary, 'Peter Pears is a dear & very sympathetic person'. Over the next months they met fairly often in London and elsewhere, attending concerts or playing tennis, but their professional and social lives did not yet much overlap. However, when Beth Britten became engaged later in the year, they decided to share a flat. After much searching, they chose one in south-west London and moved in during March 1938.

In the meantime, with some £2,000 inherited from his mother, the composer had bought an old Suffolk mill house at Snape, near Aldeburgh, with 'a grand view and alot [sic][(2)] of land to ensure its not being built round', and arranged for it to be converted into a quiet dwelling conducive to composition. There would be a big studio for himself and another ṣmaller one for Lennox Berkeley, who had agreed to share the running costs. Britten now composed his *Variations on a Theme of Frank Bridge* for string orchestra in response to an urgent commission from the conductor Boyd Neel, writing it quickly and earning Neel's delighted praise for 'one of the most astonishing feats of composition in my experience'. Though he did not attend the work's first public performance in the Salzburg Mozarteum on 27 August (it had already been broadcast), Peter Pears made a detour from a continental holiday to be there and wrote to him that night:

The Old Mill House at Snape, near Aldeburgh, photographed in the late 1930s.

'Well, Benjie, I have dashed back to the hotel...I think there can be no doubt about it that the Variations were a great success...I got a *very* strong impression that the Variations were the most *interesting* work in the programme...It really was a grand show. I'll write some more in the morning, & see if I can get any press cuttings, & then I'll air mail it to you.'

The next morning Pears added a note and a cutting from the *Salzburger Volksblatt* that referred to the new work as

'quite splendid...One is accustomed in mid-Europe to approach English music with cool reserve – often wrongly in the opinion of the English. On this occasion, however, a brilliant performance placed the pieces in the proper light and thus there was much atmosphere and great applause, which visibly brought pleasure to the sympathetic young artists.'

At around this same time, Pears sang in two more Britten compositions. One was the music for a radio programme called *The Company of Heaven* in which the BBC Singers took part and he had a solo. The other was a set of five songs to poems by Auden to which Britten gave the title *On This Island*. On 15 October, Pears and the composer ran through the songs for Lennox Berkeley and Christopher Isherwood, and Britten wrote in his diary, 'Peter sings them well – if he studies he will be a very good singer. He's certainly one of the nicest people I know, but frightfully reticent'. This astute comment reminds us that Pears, though three years older than Britten, had as yet barely begun a solo career and was deeply uncertain of his technique and potential. It is harder to know how insecure Britten still felt. Marjorie Fass noted how he showed Frank Bridge the new Auden songs, evidently expecting approval, and then became 'spoilt young Benjy in a silent temper' on not getting it. Bridge, in his turn, told her that he would never again try to help his former pupil. She commented shrewdly:

'I know he is in a mental muddle abt a great deal & dreads the future, so I had to go & put my arms about him & give him a good hug & he said 'thank you, Marj, that was nice of you'. He really hates growing up & away from a very happy childhood that ended only with his Mother's death...'

Britten now suffered from occasional fainting spells, and accepted his doctor's orders to stay in bed over Christmas 1937. His heart was checked and found to be normal, but clearly he was in poor health and his friends urged him to give up his lifestyle of late nights and early rising. However, he still felt a driving energy, and in April 1938, shortly after setting up his London base with Pears, he moved in to his Old Mill at Snape to start work on a new piece. This was a four-movement Piano Concerto for him to perform under the baton of Sir Henry Wood in the 1938 Promenade Concerts; he dedicated it to Lennox Berkeley, who stayed at Snape during May.

Though Berkeley was now deeply attached to Britten, the younger man avoided a special commitment, and younger male protégés figured in his life at this time. There was Piers Dunkerley, an English schoolboy of 17 whom he called 'my foster child', a younger boy from a poor London family whom he took on holiday to Cornwall, and a Basque lad of about 12: he was Andoni Barrutia, a refugee from the Spanish Civil War to whom Britten offered a home at Snape, writing, 'I am enjoying the responsibility tremendously'. But these relationships were short-lived: Dunkerley was growing up and a fortnight of the London boy proved a 'slight over-dose'. As for the unfortunate Barrutia, who spoke no English and must have been deeply lonely, he enjoyed only twelve days of his 'adoption', for after experiencing servant problems Britten returned him to his refugee camp, writing, 'Andoni is going – which bleeds my heart but it is better on the whole'. The composer's sister Beth Welford, who escorted Andoni back to London, later wrote of this incident, 'It was really a hopeless idea'.

23

Wolfgang (Wulff) Scherchen
at the Old Mill towards the
end of the 1930s.

A more fruitful and lasting relationship was with Wolfgang (Wulff) Scherchen, the son of the German conductor Hermann Scherchen. Four years before, Britten had met him in Florence, aged 14 and staying with his family at the same pension during the ISCM Festival, and shared a mackintosh with him when caught by a sudden rainstorm. He remembered the boy's charm and personality, and in June 1938, hearing that Wulff was living with his mother in Cambridge, he invited him to visit The Old Mill and the boy spent a weekend with him during the following month. Britten wanted him to attend the Prom première of his *Piano Concerto* on 18 August, but as Wulff was to be abroad with his father, urged him not to miss the broadcast of the concert and 'listen in hard...it is a thousand pities that you can't be there – at least I think it is!' (He heard it on the radio in Strasbourg.) Evidently Britten linked the Concerto with Wulff's joyous youthfulness, for before the concert Berkeley told him in a letter, 'If music be indeed the food of love, I think you stand a very good chance', while Auden wired, 'Vive la musique à bas les femmes', and asked, 'what about its effect on a certain person of importance?'.

Britten's Piano Concerto is a work of splashy virtuosity and extrovert brashness. Indeed, in a programme note for the première the composer called it 'a bravura work' and declared that its goose-stepping march finale offered 'a somewhat jingoistic dialogue...a feeling of doubt creeps into the music...[finally] the orchestra shouts the march in all its swagger...and the music rushes headlong to its confident finish'. He received a fee of eight guineas for playing it. Writing in *The Listener*, the composer and critic Constant Lambert called his performance brilliant but felt that the third and fourth movements lacked direction, while *The Times* wondered if the composer was writing tongue-in-cheek. For Frank Bridge, the work was simply disappointing, and Marjorie Fass was scathing: 'of *music* and originality there is no trace...If Benjy develops some day later on, he will see the insignificance of this work'. The ever curious Auden soon demanded to meet Wulff Scherchen, who remembered the poet as making him drink brandy. The young German preferred Peter Pears, and, interestingly, thought him 'a wonderful father figure' to the composer: 'He was the wise man in the background [and] had this air of stability that Ben didn't have...[a] quiet, steadying influence' – and thus quite the opposite of Auden. Indeed, Britten seems at this time to have needed both Auden's stimulus and Pears's reassurance. Later, Auden's influence waned, while Pears's affectionately paternal role was to last: some of his letters to Britten even begin, 'My boy'. (Someone who knew them well in later years, the Aldeburgh Festival manager Stephen Reiss, says that 'it was as if he was in the role of parent to a gifted and wilful child', adding, however, that when they quarrelled it was usually Pears who conceded.)

In the meantime, the careers of Pears and Britten still moved independently, and the tenor, who had left the BBC Singers in 1937, now relied on other work including a few solo engagements. Although they were later to become a celebrated recital duo, this was still some time in the future and the date of their first concert has proved elusive. Pears was to recall one in 1937 in aid of a fund for Spanish war relief. However, their first documented joint engagement was on 17 February 1939, at Balliol College, Oxford. At the end of 1938, Britten and Pears moved to another London flat at 67 Hallam Street, near Broadcasting House. But as 1939 began and war clouds gathered over Europe, both men became increasingly restless, as Pears later remembered:

'It was really in '38 that Ben began to feel that he wasn't doing much good, although he had actually done quite well...And in '39, Ben and I decided that he was not getting anywhere fast enough, as it were...He was dissatisfied, he wanted to get away from Europe and the approaching war. We were both pacifists, and we didn't see ourselves doing very much...Ben had an offer of a film in Hollywood and I decided that I'd go off with him to America.'

Pears had already visited the US twice with the New English Singers and was enthusiastic about the country and its New World freshness and promise. Though the film music offer fell through, they stuck to their plan of leaving in April 1939, preceded by Auden and Isherwood. Before leaving, Britten also confided to a woman friend, Enid Slater, that he wanted to distance himself from a relationship that had become difficult; perhaps this was the one with Wulff Scherchen, but the friendship with Berkeley also worried him. Neither he nor Pears were sure how long they would stay away, but while Pears expected to return to England in August, Britten wrote to tell an American composer friend, Aaron Copland, that he hoped for 'a job or two to stay the Autumn'.

Britten and Pears held an eve-of-departure 'drop-in' party at their flat at which the guests included Barbara Britten and Beth Welford (with her husband and baby) and Ralph Hawkes.

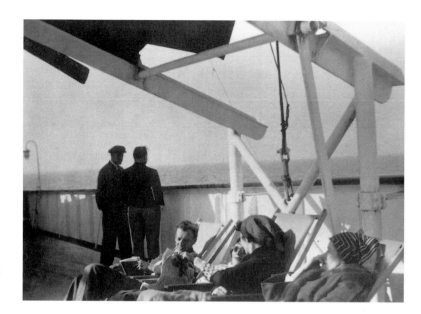

Benjamin Britten on board
the *SS Ausonia* in 1939.

When they reached Southampton on 29 April, Britten was
pleased to find that the Bridges had driven over from their
Sussex home to say goodbye – 'darned nice of them', he
commented. As they boarded the Cunard White Star liner
SS Ausonia, Bridge, a viola player like Britten himself, stepped
forward and presented his viola to his old pupil. Since he was to
die in 1941, they did not meet again. Britten and Pears stayed
on the North American continent for nearly three years.

(1) 1934 also saw the deaths of Delius and Holst.

(2) Britten habitually joined article to noun when writing
    the words 'a bit' and 'a lot'.

26

Chapter 3

America

Britten found the ten-day Atlantic crossing boring, but noted that 'the old ladies adored' a recital Pears and he gave. Characteristically, he was already having second thoughts about his trip, and told Wulff Scherchen, whose photo was on his cabin table, 'What a fool one is to come away' – though that may not have been quite sincere. Their ship reached Quebec on 9 May and then went on to Montreal; there his first engagement was a meeting with the Canadian Broadcasting Corporation, who commissioned from him a work for piano and string orchestra which he eventually called *Young Apollo* – and which was inspired by Wulff Scherchen, to whom he wrote, underlined, 'you know whom that's written about'.

Britten and Pears then stayed for a while in a hill resort, where the composer worked on this newly commissioned piece, a *Violin Concerto* and yet another orchestral work, based on local melodies, that later became his *Canadian Carnival*. After that, he was ready to move on to New York, where he was to meet the Boosey & Hawkes representative Hans Heinsheimer and contact Auden and Aaron Copland. But he also worried about how he would like the city, and how world events might develop, writing to Enid Slater on 27 June during his train journey:

Britten with Aaron Copland (centre) and Peter Pears, in upstate New York in 1939.

'As you see we are on the way...We had a terrific time in Toronto & really met some charming people...& I've been asked to write a special work [he was to perform *Young Apollo* with the CBC orchestra on 27 August].

'I'm looking forward to New York. But also feeling abit nervous about it – with all its sophistication & 'New Yorker' brightness. I can't do that sort of thing very well. However I hope we'll find a nice place to settle down in for abit – near Cape Cod or Boston – I want to do some more work. No plans for the Autumn yet – even as far as one can possibly plan these days. Things of course look very black to us out here...Here, I'm afraid, one is inclined to speak of Europe in the past tense. I think it *may* be this side of the Atlantic for me – but it is impossible to say as yet – because lots of things will have to be got over before that decision is made.'

However, by now he had made a momentous decision concerning his private life. Hitherto, he and Pears had been close friends, but, while visiting the Michigan city of Grand Rapids in mid-June, they became lovers in the physical sense. A few months later, Pears was to tell him in a letter, 'I shall never forget a certain night in Grand Rapids. Ich liebe dich...I'm terribly in love with you', and over three decades later he again declared, 'it is *you* who have given *me* everything, right from the beginning, from yourself in Grand Rapids!'. For some time, Britten kept this private, but he was evidently elated and wrote to tell Lennox Berkeley, 'We had a terrific time in Grand Rapids'. He also told Berkeley proudly of his Canadian successes, which included several press interviews ('They think I'm pretty hot out here & I'm not trying to disillusion them!'), a broadcast of his *Frank Bridge Variations* and a broadcast recital of his songs given by Pears.

Thus it was that the person who finally replaced Britten's mother as central in his affections was, like her, a singer, and inevitably, his future artistic development reflected this. Beth Welford believed that her brother's 'chief creative power was writing for the voice, and there was something about Peter's voice which gave Ben what he needed'; and she agreed with someone who remarked that this voice resembled her mother's. Not surprisingly, living with Britten transformed this formerly diffident and unambitious singer, who now worked intensively to improve his technique and interpretative range. Britten, evidently responding, composed a new song cycle called *Les illuminations*, and though Sophie Wyss was to give its première (in London on 30 January 1940), Pears later sang it in New York, on 12 May 1941, during the New York Festival of the International Society for Contemporary Music. The composer told Sophie Wyss that he did so beautifully, and that one day they would compare their two readings. Much later, in 1967, he was to say in a radio interview:

'The only thing which moves me about singers...is that the voice is something that comes naturally from their personality, and is a vocal expression of that personality. I loathe what is normally called 'a beautiful voice', because to me it's like an overripe peach, which says nothing.'

Though Britten's long-term plans remained uncertain during this summer of 1939, he told Beth on 25 June:

'It looks as if I shall stay over here – unless there's a war. I might as well confess it now, that I am seriously considering staying over here permanently. I haven't decided yet of course and I'm terribly torn, but I admit that if a definite offer turned up (and there are several in the air) I might take it. Use your judgement as to whether you tell anyone. As it is so much in the air I suggest you don't...I am *certain* that N. America is the place of the future.'

In fact, Britten and Pears stayed only a few nights in New York. They then went on to stay near Aaron Copland and his friend Victor Kraft at Woodstock, near the Catskill Mountains but still within reach of the city. They spent most of July and August there, Britten's work being 'rather inspired by such sunshine as I've never seen before', but travelled to New York for a successful performance of the *Frank Bridge Variations* on 12 July, given to an audience of several thousand in New York's open-air Lewisohn Stadium. Despite these pleasant events, Britten anxiously observed the darkening European situation as the prospect of war became stronger. Copland persuaded him to stay in the USA, whatever might happen. As for Pears, who had a return passage booked for 23 August, he decided to cancel it and also remain at least for the time being.

Towards the end of August, the two Englishmen paid a weekend visit to Pears's friend Elizabeth Mayer, a cultured German whom he had met three years before. Now in her fifties, she was married to a half-Jewish psychiatrist who had fled from Hitler's Germany and now practised at Amityville on Long Island. When war was declared on 3 September, 'mother said, "stay with us"', as her daughter Beata Sauerlander later recalled, and the two musicians accepted and so became part of the household. 'It was rather a small cottage and we were four children', says Beata; 'To this day, I don't know how we all fitted in.'

Passionately devoted to the arts, Elizabeth Mayer, according to Beth Welford, 'loved Ben from the start...she looked after him like a mother and did her best to take the place of the mother he had lost'. By early 1940, Mrs Mayer was writing to him as 'My darling' and he was signing his reply 'Your very loving Benjamin'. He called her 'one of those grand people who have been essential through the ages for the production of art; really sympathetic and enthusiastic, with instinctive good taste (in all the arts) & a great

Elizabeth Mayer, photographed in the early 1940s.

friend of thousands of those poor fish – artists. She is never happy unless she has them all round her.' She was equally attached to Pears, who also saw her as a mother figure. As for the relationship between the two men, her son Michael has said, 'My mother was never aware of such things. My mother thought that Beata ought to marry Ben, you see; but she lived in another world.' Through Britten, Auden soon became another favourite. Michael and the other younger Mayers, now adults or nearly so, showed no jealousy of the Englishmen, and the mild-mannered Dr William Mayer also unquestioningly accepted their presence in his household.

Britten and Pears photographed at the Mayer family home on Long Island, Amityville.

Thanks to his publishers, Britten's music was now receiving performances on both sides of the Atlantic. In London, Sophie Wyss sang *Les illuminations,* and in New York, in March 1940, the new *Violin Concerto* was played by Antonio Brosa and the New York Philharmonic Orchestra under John Barbirolli. Two months later, the BBC broadcast *Canadian Carnival.* Another work from this year was the *Diversions* for piano (left hand) and orchestra, written for the one-armed Austrian pianist Paul Wittgenstein; he proved hard to satisfy but was finally pleased with the piece and the composer called it 'not deep – but quite pretty!' (It received its première on 16 January 1942, with Wittgenstein and the Philadelphia Orchestra under Eugene Ormandy.) Britten also worked on a symphony in response to a commission from the Japanese government, the *Sinfonia da Requiem.* However, the Japanese rejected it as too Christian, and its first performance was in the USA on 30 March 1941, again with Barbirolli and the New York Philharmonic.

Despite a title suggesting acceptance and religious calm, and the dedication 'In memory of my parents', the *Sinfonia da Requiem* is extraordinarily passionate. Britten said in a *New York Sun* interview that it was 'just as anti-war as possible' and that the wild Dies Irae second movement was a 'Dance of Death'; yet at the same time there was much of his private self in the music and elsewhere he called it 'so personal & intimate a piece, that it is rather like those awful dreams where one parades about the place naked.' His Violin Concerto is also unconventional, ending as it does in an elegiac mood rather than with conventional virtuoso display. The melancholy of both works evidently reflects the despair from which he now sometimes suffered, and which his friends found hard to understand. The Mayers' friend David Rothman remembered that he talked wildly about giving up music altogether: 'I told him, keep going. Look, you're only about 26 years old. You've already done well...What do you want, blood?'. Beata Sauerlander says that, on one occasion,

'he was in the blackest of moods...he had a sort of block. And Mother suggested he go out to Jones Beach, a long road along the sea, miles and miles, and it was in winter and it was perfectly empty. And he drove like mad – she never forgot it, she was so scared – he drove at enormous speed, for hours, up and down that long, long stretch along the beach. And they went home, and the next morning Mother came and said, 'He is writing again.''

Britten and Pears on Jones
Beach, Long Island.

A contemporary cover for the
Seven Sonnets of Michelangelo.

As at Gresham's School, Britten's unhappiness often turned psychosomatically to illness. When he contracted a throat infection early in 1940, Beata Mayer nursed him, and, according to Pears, saved his life. Pears himself was now devoted to his friend's welfare, and revealingly, Britten wrote to tell his old friend John Pounder, 'Peter looks after me like a lover', and described him to Wulff Scherchen as 'like a mother hen'. To Beata Mayer, he said, 'Peter is a rock'.

While this situation suited Britten, and evidently Pears also, it alerted the shrewd Wystan Auden, who was later to write a remarkable letter to the composer, explaining the dangers of over-protected cosiness. But Britten had no inclination to heed such advice. He liked to be loved and admired by people whose loyalty was absolute – and who were not forgiven if it wavered. Auden was in time to learn that his friendship was easily lost, although as yet they remained close. However, almost imperceptibly, Pears was starting to replace the poet as Britten's mentor, taking over aesthetic and intellectual ground which had been Auden's undisputed territory. In the summer of 1940, Britten composed for him the passionate *Seven Sonnets of Michelangelo*, settings for tenor and piano of love poems by the Italian artist, although it was to be two years before the two men gave the first public performance.

In 1940, however, Auden's relationship with both men remained close. They visited him in Massachusetts in August, and he and Britten began their collaboration there on an operetta called *Paul Bunyan*. A few weeks later, Britten and

32

Pears left the Mayers so as to be nearer to New York and to Auden, taking a room in a Brooklyn house which the poet and his American boyfriend Chester Kallman shared with a group of fellow artists. As it turned out, this move was not really successful. Although the bohemian atmosphere and frequent parties could be fun, the house was dirty and disorganised, and one Mayer friend was shocked when the door was opened to her by a naked man. Britten soon realised that a family atmosphere had suited him better, and wrote, 'Living is quite pleasant here when it is not too exciting, but I find it almost impossible to work, and retire to Amityville at least once a week'.

Though living with Auden tested Britten, he threw himself whole-heartedly into the creation of *Paul Bunyan,* written for students of Columbia University. Auden's brilliantly chosen subject was America herself, and the clearing of her primeval forests to make room for modern society with all its blessings and blemishes; as for Bunyan himself, he was the benevolent giant who helped man establish himself while foreseeing what he must do. For Britten, this myth of innocence and experience had an obvious appeal. Yet despite the wit and depth of the libretto, the evocative music, and a skilful production in May 1941, *Bunyan* flopped with the New York music critics, with *Time* magazine summing up their view in calling it *'an anemic operetta put up by two British expatriates'.* Not surprisingly, Britten felt wounded and, although he and Auden agreed on some changes, they failed to implement them and he then withdrew the piece from his catalogue of works.[1] At the time, he declared, 'I feel that I have learned lots about what not to write for the theatre'– and, perhaps, never again to be subordinate to a librettist. The failure of this 'American' work undermined his desire to work in what was then still called the New World and from now on he thought more often of his native England.

In the meantime, he wanted an immediate change of scene, and drove with Pears to California in their 10-year-old Model T Ford to stay with the British musicians Ethel Bartlett and Rae Robertson, a married piano duo for whom he was to write his *Scottish Ballad* for pianos and orchestra as well as a shorter *Mazurka elegiaca.* This was also the time of his *First String Quartet,* composed in response to a commission from Mrs Elizabeth Sprague Coolidge, a well-known patroness of music. The Coolidge Quartet premièred this in Los Angeles in September, while the *Scottish Ballad* was first heard two months later, with Bartlett and Robertson partnered by the Cincinnati

Britten in California in 1941.

Symphony Orchestra under Eugene Goossens. Both works are witty and intelligent, yet sometimes oddly bustling and restless, and a *Los Angeles Times* reviewer thought that the Quartet's slow movement might be called 'In Memoriam for a Lost World'.

Britten's attention now focused on his discovery of the Suffolk poet George Crabbe, whose work he and Pears read after seeing an article on him in the BBC's journal *The Listener* for 29 May 1941. A reprint of a radio talk by E.M. Forster, it began with the words, 'To talk about Crabbe is to talk about England.' Some 20 years later, Britten declared that:

'it was in California in the unhappy summer of 1941 that, coming across a copy of the Poetical Works of George Crabbe in a Los Angeles bookshop, I first read his poem, *Peter Grimes*; and, at the same time, reading a most perceptive and revealing article about it by E.M. Forster, I suddenly realised where I belonged and what I lacked.'

In Crabbe's poem *The Borough*, set in a town modelled on Aldeburgh, where he lived for 30 years, Peter Grimes is a cruel fisherman who mistreats a hapless boy apprentice who then dies, as do two more who succeed him: finally Grimes himself expires in delirium and torment. Encouraged by Pears, whose literary taste was considerable, Britten saw that Grimes might become an operatic character, who, while no hero, could still be presented sympathetically. By 29 July, he had mentioned Grimes in a letter to Elizabeth Mayer as a possible operatic subject. Also, according to Pears, reading Forster's article and Crabbe's poem 'induced a tremendous nostalgia in Ben and we then and there decided that we must go home, and...we almost immediately started to apply for a passage home, which was not at all easy to get in those days.' Britten now declared, in a letter to Mrs Coolidge dated 18 October:

'I have made up my mind to return to England, at anyrate [sic] for the duration of the war. I am not telling people, because it sounds a little heroic, which it is far from being; it is really that I cannot be separated any longer from all my friends and family – going through all they are – and I'm afraid will be in the future. I think I shall be able to continue with my work over there, which is what I most want to do, of course. I don't actually know when I shall be sailing, since boats are so scarce & heavily booked up – and anyhow I have so much to get finished here, so I may not be leaving much before Christmas.'

Homesickness aside, Britten's decision to return to England may have been compounded by other factors. There had been some fall in his American income, and he received no fee for conducting his *Sinfonia da Requiem* and playing his *Piano Concerto* in Chicago; nor did Pears when he sang *Les illuminations* there. But that was not all. *Paul Bunyan* had been badly received, and some Americans were now making discouraging remarks about his music: thus, the Chicago conductor Frederick Stock thought the *Sinfonia da Requiem* had 'more manner than matter'. He was troubled, too, that some people in wartime Britain thought him unpatriotic for staying in America, although the British Embassy had advised him to do so. Overall, he was once again uneasy and uncertain.[2] Later, he was to say, 'My recollection of this time was of complete incapacity to work...I was in quite a psychological state then.'

Thus it was that when Britten and Pears returned from California in September, it was to the comforting Mayers and not to Auden's Brooklyn ménage. Someone who saw them at this time (a student called Charlie Miller) remembers that while Elizabeth Mayer and Peter Pears often laughed, Britten remained melancholy and passive, with a 'pale, patient face' – though he still recognised in the Englishmen 'a happily married couple' and that Pears 'loomed large over his Benjy.' And even here there was something to unsettle the composer. Britten had become smitten by David Rothman's teenage son Bobby (who remained unaware of his feelings), and it probably worried him

David Rothman and his teenage son, Bobby.

to recognise that his love for Pears could not change his attraction to young boys. He stayed briefly with the Rothmans and helped behind the counter of their hardware store, offering to give up music and work there, which Peter Pears told me was because he was 'in love' with Bobby. At least he could express his feelings in music, making an arrangement of a tune called 'The trees they grow so high' and dedicating it to the boy; one line is, 'You've tied me to a boy when you know he is too young'.

Britten with the conductor Serge Koussevitzsky in Boston in 1942.

On 6 January 1942, the conductor Serge Koussevitzsky and his Boston Symphony Orchestra performed Britten's *Sinfonia da Requiem*. The composer was present, and Koussevitzsky asked him why he had not yet composed an opera. Britten explained that he planned an opera based on Crabbe's narrative poem *Peter Grimes*, but could not yet afford to undertake such a large project even if a performance were guaranteed. This prompted the conductor to reach a far-sighted and momentous decision, as Britten wrote in 1945: 'Some weeks later we met again, when he told me that he had arranged for the commissioning of the opera, which was to be dedicated to the memory of his wife, who had recently died.' The commissioning fee was $1000, a decent sum in those days although hardly overwhelming.

Having decided to return to Britain, Britten and Pears now awaited exit permits and passages and began a series of goodbyes. Wystan Auden wrote to say that he regretted their going, and Elizabeth Mayer was increasingly distressed as their sailing date of 16 March 1942 approached – 'The Ides of March', she noted in her diary. Typically, Britten now had second thoughts, just as he had had when he left England three years before: 'How I wish I weren't going – there are so many people I love here', he wrote in a letter of 10 March. Pears, always the more sanguine, wrote in the same letter 'April is such a marvellous month. Think of seeing real spring again' – but Britten added, 'life in England isn't going to be fun.'

As usual, Auden aimed to have the last word. In his letter to Britten of 31 January, already referred to above, he wrote:

'Perhaps I can't make myself believe that you are really leaving us. I need scarcely say, my dear, how much I shall miss you and Peter, or how much I love you both.

'There is a lot I want to talk to you about, but I must try and say a little of it by letter. I have been thinking a great deal about you and your work during the past year. As you know I think you the white hope of music; for this very reason I am more critical of you than anybody else, and I think I know something about the dangers that beset you as a man and as an artist because they are my own.

'Goodness and beauty are the results of a perfect balance between Order and Chaos, Bohemianism and Bourgeois Convention.

'Bohemian chaos alone ends in a mad jumble of beautiful scraps; Bourgeois convention alone ends in large unfeeling corpses.

'Every artist except the supreme ones has a bias one way or the other. The best pair of opposites I can think of in music are Wagner and Strauss. (Technical skill always comes from the bourgeois side of one's nature.)

'For middle-class Englishmen like you and me, the danger is of course the second. Your attraction to thin-as-a-board juveniles, i.e. to the sexless and inocent, is a symptom of this. And I am certain too that it is your denial and evasion of the demands [the word 'attractions' is crossed out] of disorder that is responsible for your attacks of ill-health, i.e. sickness is your substitute for the Bohemian.

'Wherever you go you are and probably always will be surrounded by people who adore you, nurse you, and praise everything you do, e.g. Elizabeth, Peter (Please show this to P to whom all this is also addressed). Up to a certain point this is fine for you, but beware. You see, Bengy dear, you are always tempted to make things too easy for yourself in this way, i.e. to build yourself a warm nest of love (of course when you get it, you find it a little stifling) by playing the lovable talented little boy.

'If you are really to develop to your full stature, you will have, I think, to suffer, and make others suffer, in ways which are totally strange to you at present, and against every conscious value that you have; i.e. you will have to say what you have never yet had the right to say – God, I'm a shit...

'All my love to you both, and God bless you.'

Though Britten's reply has not survived, it is evident that he did so from a second Auden letter, which reads:

'I write at once to correct a misunderstanding. Of course I didn't mean to suggest that your relationship was on the school boy level. Its danger is quite the reverse, of you both letting the marriage be too caring. (The escape for the paederast is that a marriage is impossible.) You understand each other so well, that you will always both be tempted to identify yourselves with each other.

'I know how tiresome it must be waiting around. I, of course, hope that the migration will finally be cancelled.'

Whether or not because of Auden's advice, a letter from Britten to his brother-in-law Kit Welford shows that he now thought seriously as to his aims:

'...I am not quite sure what will happen to me. I have certain things that I want to do & which I may or may not be able to do...luckily, I believe in my work, and so don't fall into the obvious dangers of half-heartedness, which so many artists feel like these days...But what really worries me now is that I have reached a definite turning point in my work, & what I most want is to be able to think & think & work & work, completely undistracted for a good period of time...I cannot tell you how much I agree with and admire your letter. I am so pleased that you have thought things out so carefully. From a different angle I have come to an identical point-of-view (re discipline & obedience) – but in art, as you know, the bias is to the other direction, that of anarchy and romantic 'freedom'. A carefully chosen discipline is the only possible course.'

[1] However, he retained an affection for *Paul Bunyan* Four years later, he recalled that 'the public seemed to find something enjoyable in the performances', and

near the end of his life, and after Auden's death, he was persuaded to revise it for a broadcast and was moved to tears on hearing it again.

(2) At around this time, Britten wrote an overture for the Cleveland Orchestra and its conductor Artur Rodzinski, but for some reason it was not played; possibly the manuscript did not even reach them. The score then remained with a music hire agency for a while and was later passed on to the New York Public Library. When it was located there in 1972, and a copy sent to the composer by one of its staff, he replied that he had 'absolutely no recollection whatsoever' of writing it and added, 'I should love to have the work destroyed, but that is a little too much to ask of you!'. In November 1983, Simon Rattle and the City of Birmingham Symphony Orchestra gave this piece its long delayed première, under the title *An American Overture*.

Chapter 4

Wartime England and *Peter Grimes*

A contemporary cover of
A Ceremony of Carols.

Leaving America somehow liberated Britten. On his voyage home, he completed two vocal works which are fresh and confident: one was a *Hymn to St Cecilia*, to an Auden poem celebrating the composer's patron saint, and the other *A Ceremony of Carols*, settings for treble voices and harp of medieval carol texts, five of them from a volume of English verse purchased when his ship stopped at Halifax, Nova Scotia. Both are sacred pieces, owing much to the English choral tradition yet far from conventional. Both, too, offer occasional musing on tribulation yet end happily, and the final carol in the *Ceremony* even makes the point that without the Fall, Christian redemption would not have been possible. Nothing could be further from the tormented utterances of the *Sinfonia da Requiem*.

One important biographer, Humphrey Carpenter, suggests that this music shows Britten 'coming to terms with his predicament'. However, the composer's own succinct explanation of the new pieces, in a letter to Elizabeth Mayer, was merely that 'one had to alleviate the boredom!' His Swedish ship *Axel Johnson* took a month to reach England, having called at several ports on the Eastern seaboard before starting the Atlantic crossing from Boston in convoy with other vessels on 31 March. It was also hazardous, since German submarines were active in the Atlantic and sometimes erroneously attacked neutral ships. This was Britten's first taste of wartime danger, enhanced when their ship's funnel caught fire and they were temporarily left unescorted. He and Pears also suffered some discomfort in their cabin facing the ship's refrigerator, which produced smells, as Pears later recalled, that were 'not at all helpful to someone suffering rather from seasickness'. But they used their time as best they could, and another fruitful piece of work on the voyage was a numbered synopsis and musical summary of Britten's projected *Peter Grimes* opera (it still exists, in Pears's handwriting); at this time there was talk of his writing the libretto, but in the end this came to nothing, for as he later said, 'I hadn't the skill or the time, really'.

Britten and Pears arrived in Britain on 17 April. Since neither man had informed his relatives of his journey, perhaps to avoid worrying them, the telegram that Britten sent to his sisters from Liverpool came as a joyful surprise. He now had much to do, not least the task of settling again in his Suffolk home, and he also hurried to see a former theatrical collaborator, Montagu Slater, his chosen librettist for *Peter Grimes*. While in America, Britten had maintained a friendly correspondence with his wife Enid, and on 4 May he wrote to tell Elizabeth Mayer:

'M. [Slater] has taken to *Grimes* like a duck to water & the opera is leaping ahead. It is very exciting – I must write & tell Koussey about it. He has splendid ideas. It is getting more and more an opera about the community, whose life is 'illuminated' for this moment by the tragedy of the murders. Ellen [the schoolmistress who befriends Grimes] is growing in importance, & there are fine minor characters, such as the Parson, pub-keeper, 'quack'-apothecary, & doctor.'

Britten's mood of elation at this time also linked to Pears's having quickly resumed his English career at a higher level than before, and in the same letter he told Mrs Mayer:

'We (P. & I) have played all the new stuff to Ralph [Hawkes] – the Michelangelo made a great impression – & on the strength of it Peter has had this *Tales of Hoffmann* offer (to sing Hoffmann) which will be splendid experience for him. He's singing *so* well, & everyone is surprised & delighted...'

Pears sang the title role in a production of Offenbach's *Tales of Hoffmann* which opened on 6 May at the Strand Theatre in London. Britten too looked set for a career advance, for the BBC executive Julian Herbage, attending the play-through for his publisher, informed his departmental head, the conductor Sir Adrian Boult, that 'one looks for most important if not great things from him in the future'.

Thus, Britten and Pears re-entered British musical life and seemingly paid no penalty for their three-year absence.

41

Imogen Holst.

However, in one respect their future was uncertain. On 28 May, Britten appeared before a tribunal to state his case for registration as a conscientious objector to warfare, and thus for exemption from military service, arguing that he could best serve his country by using his creative skill and declaring, 'I cannot take part in acts of destruction'. The tribunal agreed to exempt him from military service but left him subject to call-up for non-combatant duties; however, he then appealed and obtained the unconditional exemption that he wanted. Pears also achieved this. Thus the two of them could now continue their careers without interruption or hindrance.

Soon Britten and Pears were again sharing London accommodation, and they now began giving joint recitals for the Council for the Encouragement of Music and the Arts (CEMA), a forerunner of the present-day Arts Council of Great Britain. Some of these occasions were 'fantastic adventures', according to their friend Imogen Holst, the daughter of the composer Gustav Holst and herself a CEMA organiser:

'They would have to find their way in the pouring rain down some dark, muddy East Anglian lane that was little better than a cart-track, until they eventually reached a desolate, tin-roofed village hall. Here they would find a smoking oil stove in one corner and in the opposite corner an elderly upright piano with polished brass candle-brackets and panels of fretwork and faded pink silk. In the middle of the hall would be an audience of twenty or thirty people who had never been to a concert before, but who were enthralled by the singing and playing.'

One such recital, at Melksham in Wiltshire, was followed by a second, shorter programme at a local school three miles away. A pupil called Claire Purdie walked to the town to hear them and then back to the school, only to find that Pears and Britten had just finished their second concert and were about to leave. She says: 'I was so upset that I marched in without thinking and told them what had happened. Whereupon BB opened the piano lid and PP sang 'Down by the Salley Gardens' just for me.' *The Salley Gardens* was one of the composer's many folk-song arrangements, a popular feature of these joint recitals.

In March 1943, the *Observer* critic William Glock showed equal satisfaction:

'Not long ago Mr Britten – who might have been Schumann or Mendelssohn a hundred years ago – played in a village hall while a small boy in the front row spent his time in seeing how far he could roll a penny along the floor before reclaiming it by stamping on it with his foot. A few days later he had introduced his *Michelangelo Sonnets* to an audience at Bishop's Stortford, who fell completely in love with them.'

Britten now reassessed his pre-war relationships. Since the outbreak of war, Wulff Scherchen had been interned and then released, perhaps because his father had been a well-known anti-Nazi; but he was now 22 and Britten found him 'altered, I am afraid...rather vindictive, and hard'. 'I shouldn't see him much', he told Pears. Lennox Berkeley, too, was less on the scene, having relinquished his interest in The Old Mill and now working for the EBC; he married in 1946 and Britten became godfather to Berkeley's eldest son Michael and remained a friend. His commitment to Pears was now absolute, and he was proud of their relationship, telling the singer in a letter how he had talked of it to a woman friend: 'I don't care who knows'.

Pears now possessed the skill and self-assurance essential for a performance of the as yet unheard *Michelangelo Sonnets*, and when he and Britten gave the première of this cycle, on 23 September 1942 in London's Wigmore Hall, the critical reaction was extremely warm. These were 'Fine songs for singing', declared *The Times*, and the *New Statesman and Nation* thought them the best since the songs of Hugo Wolf. The performers were immediately asked to record the work, and did so on 20 November for His Master's Voice (now EMI). Pears told Elizabeth Mayer:

'We have recorded the *Michelangelo* for HMV and they have sold enormously. It is remarkable (or isn't it remarkable, Elizabeth) how much everyone loves the *Sonnets*. We do them to very simple audiences & all say it is what they have been waiting for. They have made a tremendously deep impression.'

It is wrong, however, to assume that all this success was easily won. People still criticised Britten's absence in the early years of the war and now branded his and Pears's pacifist stand as cowardly, or at best intended to protect their careers at a time when others of their generation had set aside their work and private lives to serve their country. Pears, whose forbears included generals and admirals, had to endure family disapproval, and a relative still remembers how his pacifism 'went down like a lead balloon with the service side'. There were inevitably also whispers as to the nature of their relationship, and a contemporary says that 'they ogled each other on stage'. In 1980, the *Daily Telegraph* critic Peter Stadlen remembered the first hearing of the *Michelangelo Sonnets* with the words, 'At the end, after a second or two of tense silence, a burst of tumultuous applause proved that music had won the day'. Evidently he sensed a degree of unease in the hall.

As for the hypersensitive Britten, he too felt it, and was later to write that, as conscientious objectors in wartime Britain, he and Pears felt themselves to be outsiders and 'experienced tremendous tension'. But his biographer Michael Kennedy takes this statement further and asks, 'Is it to be seriously doubted that "and homosexuals" were unspoken but implied words in that statement?'. Kennedy must be right. The composer's setting of the love poems that Michelangelo addressed to his *'signior mio'* could well have been thought audacious, especially when the cycle was dedicated to his singer. Humphrey Carpenter considers that this song cycle was widely seen 'as a public announcement of his involvement with Pears'. If Britten intended this to be so, which remains doubtful, this was brave indeed for a young man with most of his career still before him: significantly, he admitted in a letter that he had been nervous and that 'it seemed cruel to parade them [the songs] in the cold light of the Wigmore Hall'. A few days after this celebrated first performance, he went down with influenza and remained ill for some weeks, his doctor concluding that he had 'practically no resistance'.

The composition of his opera *Peter Grimes* was also courageous, for here was an enormous undertaking both artistically and in terms of sheer hard work. In 1945, he was to write that it had involved 'the construction of a scenario, discussions with a librettist, planning the musical architecture, composing preliminary sketches, and writing nearly a thousand pages of orchestral score'. As we have seen, his collaboration with Montagu Slater went well at first, and he told his librettist's wife, 'the more I think of *P. Grimes* the more I like it & get excited over it.' But Slater was a slow writer, and in due course the composer became unhappy with his scenario, considering it insufficiently clear as to Grimes's nature: 'no reasons & not many symptoms! He's got to be changed alot.' He also resisted his librettist's wish to turn the story into a left-wing tract, with Grimes's harsh ambition represented as natural to bourgeois society, and briefly even considered dropping him altogether.

But these obstacles were overcome: the libretto was completed by the end of 1943 and Britten began sustained work on his score in January 1944.

Clearly the new opera should have a role for Peter Pears. Having joined the Sadler's Wells Opera Company in January 1943, Pears was now touring Britain and singing leading roles in such operas as *The Magic Flute, La bohème, La traviata, Rigoletto* and *Così fan tutte*. Britten saw most of these productions and marvelled at his friend's blossoming gifts. Others, too, were struck by the tenor's intelligence and sheer musicianship; among them was the critic Hans Keller, who saluted him as 'A singer who isn't a poor substitute for an instrumentalist! A voice of character which carries farther and deeper than any voice thrice as strong!...He does not merely act well. He instinctively acts the music'. Britten also admired Pears's triumphant performance, in

Pears as Ferrando in a Sadler's Wells production of *Così fan tutte*, with Margaret Ritchie as Dorabella.

October 1943, of his latest song cycle, the lyrical yet dramatic *Serenade* for tenor, horn and strings. Between them, these two men were making people feel, as the composer wrote to Imogen Holst,

"something' in the air that heralds a renaissance...It is so very exciting. It is of course in all the arts, but in music, particularly, it's this acceptance of freedom without any arbitrary restrictions, this simplicity, this contact with audiences of our own time and of people like ourselves, this seriousness, and above all this professionalism.'

Originally, Britten had intended that the role of Peter Grimes would be sung by a baritone, the 'heavier' kind of voice traditionally given to villains or older men, just as tenors sang young heroes. But Grimes was no longer villainous: instead, as Pears put it in a letter to the composer, the lonely fisherman had become 'an introspective, an artist, a neurotic, his real problem is expression, self-expression...What a part! Wow!' By April 1943, Britten knew that he wanted Pears to portray his protagonist and told William Mayer, 'I hope he'll do the principal part in *Peter Grimes.'*

Though Koussevitzsky's commission had anticipated that *Peter Grimes* would be first seen in America, in the event he did not insist on this. That meant that a native cast could create this very British work, and Britten was grateful. In an interview, he declared:

'I am passionately interested in seeing a successful permanent national opera in existence – successful both artistically and materially. And it must be vital and contemporary, too, and depend less on imported 'stars' than on a first-rate, young and fresh, permanent company. Sadler's Wells have made a good beginning.'

The Sadler's Wells Opera Company's artistic director was the soprano Joan Cross. Born in 1900, she had sung in opera since 1924 and been a principal with the company since 1936, assuming her directorship seven years later; Pears had worked with her teacher, Dawson Freer, and admired her artistry. Encouraged by Pears, Cross took an interest in the making of *Peter Grimes,* and Britten then played the Prologue and Act 1 to her and some of her colleagues, the administrator Tyrone Guthrie, the conductor Lawrance Collingwood and the young producer Eric Crozier. She later recalled: 'It made the most terrific impression. I think I wasn't alone in my immediate reaction,

A page from the composer's autograph manuscript of *Peter Grimes*.

that this was the piece to reopen Sadler's Wells [whose theatre in London had closed for the duration] when the finish of the war came.' Sadler's Wells now decided to mount the new production, for which CEMA made some public funds available. As for the date of the première, it depended on the ending of the European hostilities, but by this time it was felt that this could not be far off.

Peter Grimes was mostly composed at Britten's Old Mill, only a few miles from Crabbe's 'Borough', Aldeburgh, and Beth Welford has given this description of her brother's working day:

'Many people have the idea that musicians, artists and writers work by inspiration frantically working while the inspiration lasts. That was not the way Benjamin worked. When he was working at home, he kept regular hours and worked to a set pattern. Always an early riser he would be in his studio at least by 9.00 a.m., working through until 1 o'clock with a break for coffee, then a light lunch and some form of exercise...he walked far and fast [and] did much of the planning...and sometimes sang as he went...After the afternoon walk and a cup of tea, Ben returned to his studio and worked again solidly for three more hours; then dinner, perhaps a read or a game, and bed. This was the pattern he followed throughout his life, when he was able to be at home, in Snape and later on in Aldeburgh.'

Though Britten needed to work quickly on *Peter Grimes*, he had problems with it. He told Pears in April 1944, '*Grimes* is being such a brute', and in June he wrote, 'My bloody opera stinks'. He was also disturbed by 'bloody, bloody' RAF aircraft from nearby bases. But he stuck at his task and finished his vocal score (containing all the notes, but not yet orchestrated) in February 1945. Then came the vast labour of completing the orchestral score, which he managed to finish a few weeks before Germany's surrender in May.

During the run-up to the première of *Peter Grimes* in London, on 7 June 1945, the Sadler's Wells Company continued to tour and from February onwards rehearsals for the new opera took place in various provincial locations. Problems soon became evident, for some singers disliked the music and one soprano was put out when the composer's insistence on having Joan Cross as Ellen Orford meant that she had no part at all. As Pears later remembered, there were 'jealousies and resentments', and great nervousness about reopening the Wells with an untried opera when previous ventures with British opera had failed. Eric Crozier, then just thirty and the producer of the

A photograph of the composer, Michael Tippett, taken in the 1940s.

new piece, could understand these attitudes and later wrote, 'There was indeed no tradition of writing opera; there was no tradition among audiences of wanting to see contemporary operas'; and Pears soon learned that many, perhaps most, of his colleagues would have preferred performing Edward German's popular opera *Merrie England*.

Thus, the decision to mount *Peter Grimes* was a bold one. Yet somehow the faith of Joan Cross and a few others in Britten's opera carried rehearsals along. Auspiciously, the première was to be a young man's night: the composer, protagonist and producer were all young, and the conductor was the company's 39-year-old répétiteur Reginald Goodall. Several London-based musicians not associated with the Wells, among them the composer Michael Tippett, then 40, attended rehearsals and went away impressed, vowing to attend the première and urging their friends to do the same. Little by little, most of the doubters among the cast came around, and the first orchestral rehearsals made a big difference to them: the storm music in Act 1, said Joan Cross, 'simply knocked you over'. Peter Pears noticed how his fellow singers finally appreciated *Grimes,* not least the members of the chorus representing the Borough community which plays such a major part:

'A lot of them were convinced by the music, and I can remember them enjoying the rehearsals, the chorus for instance really loved to have something to sing, and in many ways it really is a chorus opera.'

The story of *Peter Grimes* is fast-moving and dramatic. At the inquest on his boy apprentice, Grimes, a rough lone fisherman, explains the death as resulting from exposure and thirst at sea, and is exonerated but advised not to take another lad into his service. Though mistrusted by the Borough, Grimes nevertheless has a friend in Ellen Orford, the schoolmistress, whom he hopes to marry when he has earned money and respect, and sympathetic acquaintances in the retired Captain Balstrode and the pub landlady 'Auntie'. Rejecting the coroner's advice, Grimes takes a second apprentice, John (a non-singing role), and soon quarrels violently with Ellen over his maltreatment of the boy. In an accident at Grimes's cliffside hut, partly precipitated by this quarrel, John slips and falls to his death. Grimes then disappears out to sea, while the community decide that he is guilty of murder and engage in a manhunt. Finally he returns at night and is found by Ellen and Balstrode. Watched despairingly by Ellen, Balstrode advises him to sail out again and drown himself. As dawn comes, and his boat is seen sinking far out at sea, the Borough resumes its daily life, and the tragedy of the fisherman and his apprentices is already being washed away and forgotten.

The set of the first production of *Peter Grimes*, Sadler's Wells, 1945.

Imogen Holst wrote of the première of *Peter Grimes*:

'No one in the audience will ever forget the excitement of that evening. Here, at last, was a real English opera that was going to live side by side with any of the great operas of the world. The drama in the music was utterly compelling from the first note to the last, and each of the characters had a musical personality. The story moved swiftly: there was no aimless hanging around, yet the singers sang real arias with memorable tunes that could be taken home and whistled. When the action needed the urgency of recitative, the sung conversations had all the directness and energy of their own native language. The huge orchestra never drowned the singers' words, yet when the east-coast storm arose the whole theatre was flooded with wave after wave of sound. Actors and audience were aware all the time of the cold, grey sea of Crabbe's poem: when a door at the back of the stage suddenly blew open at the height of the storm, Suffolk listeners sitting in the stalls could feel the north-east draught round their ankles. The music stretched beyond the boxed-in sides of the stage, and when the hostile crowds in the wings called out 'Peter Grimes!...*Peter Grimes!*', their voices sounded as if they were coming from far along the coast. In the fog of the terrible man-hunt, the poor demented fisherman seemed to grow in stature until he was no longer a separate individual:...he was bearing the burden of all those other outcasts who are rejected by their law-abiding neighbours because they are different from other people. When the tragedy had reached its quiet end and the opera was over, the listeners knew that they had been hearing a masterpiece, and that nothing like this had ever happened before in English music. They stood up and shouted and shouted.'

Next day, there were the papers. The *Daily Express* characteristically went for human interest and described the composer rather than the opera itself: 'A slim, curly-haired young man in evening dress stood for three hours at the back of the stalls in Sadler's Wells Theatre last night, too nervous to sit down. At the end he took an ovation from an audience containing some of the greatest names in music.'[1]

The broadsheets had more to say, most of it favourable. *The Times* found it 'a good omen for English opera that this first-fruit of peace should declare decisively that opera on the grand scale and in the grand manner can still be written.' In the *Daily Telegraph*, Ferruccio Bonavia wrote, 'This opera has force, vitality, beauty' although it had 'neither love-duet, nor hero'. The *Birmingham Post* critic Eric Blom thought it 'gloomy, harrowing and depressing', but still judged it 'a work of genius...so impressive and original that only the most absurd prejudice will keep it out of the great foreign opera houses.' In the *Observer*, William Glock also used the word 'genius' and concluded, 'Don't miss it.' Finally, in three successive *Sunday Times* articles, the doyen of British music critics, the 76-year-old Ernest Newman, called *Peter Grimes* 'the most important new work of the year' and summed up:

'The whole texture, musical and dramatic, of the opera is admirably unified, in spite of the many genres it employs, ranging from almost naked speech to music at its fullest power; but to listen to it in the right way the spectator must approach it from its own standpoint, not that of any previous operatic species.'

Reading these tributes to *Peter Grimes*, we should still remember that some critics had reservations. *Time & Tide* thought that the opera failed to make sufficiently explicit its theme of its hero's divided nature, 'which is finally the sole claim on dramatic interest'. The *Evening News* missed 'a large abundance of the spirit, over and above technique [despite] a few moments of heartfelt beauty'. One reaction, by Geoffrey Sharp in his journal *Music Review*, was truly hostile. For him, its composer was 'afraid to develop a lyrical vein and reluctant to express in his music any emotional conflict.' Yet his was a lone voice.

Peter Pears in the title role
of Peter Grimes.

Thus the production of *Peter Grimes*, occurring as it did in the heady excitement of the recent European victory, was a triumph, and not only for the composer. Peter Pears's portrayal of Grimes was widely acclaimed, as was Joan Cross's Ellen, and indeed all concerned could congratulate themselves that the risk of staging this new work had been taken and had more than paid off. Later in that month of June, Britten wrote to Imogen Holst:

Joan Cross in the role of the
schoolmistress, Ellen Orford.

'I am so glad that the opera came up to your expectations...I must confess that I am very pleased with the way that it seems to 'come over the footlights', and also with the way the audience takes it, and what is perhaps more, returns night after night to take it again! I think the occasion is actually a greater one than either Sadler's Wells or me. Perhaps it is an omen for English Opera in the future. Anyhow, I hope that many composers will take the plunge, and I hope also that they'll find, as I did, the water not quite so icy as expected!'

What Peter Pears later called the 'impetus' of *Peter Grimes* took it on a rapid conquest of the European and American opera houses. Within three years it had been translated into seven languages and been produced in Stockholm, Basle, Antwerp, Zurich, Tanglewood (under the young Leonard Bernstein), Milan, Hamburg, Mannheim, Berlin, Brno, Graz, Copenhagen, Budapest and New York – where *Time* devoted an article to '*Britain's Britten*'. It gave its composer worldwide fame.

It is worth putting these artistic events in a wider context. On 8 June 1945, the day following the first night of *Peter Grimes*, the London papers' news items, advertisements and the like all characterise the time, place and social structure. Field-Marshal Montgomery received the freedom of the City of Antwerp, while William Joyce, who had broadcast for the Nazis and earned the nickname of 'Lord Haw-Haw', had been arrested (he was later executed for treason). There was a food shortage in London, and housewives were told how to 're-register' their new ration books and advised to purchase sweets at local shops where they were known. Peaches were available to the wealthy at several shillings each, but the children's allowance for servicemen's families was just five shillings (25p) per week. At Sotheby's someone paid £72 for a silver tobacco box, and Mackinlay's Scotch Whisky cost 25/9d a bottle. Bakelite Plastics Ltd announced that 'furniture of the future will owe a great deal to Plastics' and Vivien Leigh was playing at London's Phoenix Theatre in Thornton Wilder's play *The Skin of our Teeth*.

Today, as the next millennium approaches, Britain has changed beyond recognition and the first production of *Peter Grimes* lies half a century in the past. We can see it more clearly than people did then, in the light of the composer's later development and of musical history overall. In fact its first critics were admirably perspicacious in seeing it as an augury of a major individual talent and a promise for the future of British music, for it revitalised opera in this country. They rightly noted its fluency, command of varied moods, dramatic immediacy and emotional force, and that its well-shaped plot was backed by a correspondingly unified musical structure. In other words, they saw that Britten was a born musical dramatist. Yet what gave *Peter Grimes* lasting success is perhaps something beyond all these things. This opera has a strikingly personal quality. The soundscape is Britten's own because its feeling is so individual, strangely wounded yet tough, defiant and coolly intelligent. Its passion and pain are not of the cardboard-theatrical kind, but ring uncomfortably true. Britten himself had said of *Grimes*, 'A central feeling for us was that of the individual against the crowd, with ironic overtones for our own situation.' Is it then a parable about persecution, with the composer and his singer as potential victims? We need not go as far as the gay British scholar Philip Brett, who sees the opera as a homosexual man's 'ultimate fantasy of persecution and suicide': this is too crude.[2]

None the less, the outsider theme was to recur in other Britten operas, such as *Albert Herring, Owen Wingrave* and *Death in Venice*, and reflects an important aspect of the composer's own makeup. The impact of *Peter Grimes* is partly due to its quasi-autobiographical intensity.

[1] Vaughan Williams attended this première, as did Walton, Berkeley, Tippett and the 29-year-old Yehudi Menuhin. John Ireland was not present, but, after hearing Britten conduct the *Four Sea Interludes* from the opera a few days later, praised his former pupil: 'In some respects he could twist every other composer in this country round his little finger.'

[2] Brett's argument, however, deserves to be quoted more fully: 'The dawning realisation of sexual feeling [in adolescence] can rarely be a simple matter; when it is homosexual feeling and the family tie is strong, the resulting conflict can be devastating – for it is the special characteristic of the homosexual stigma (unlike that attached to being black or Jewish) that it is almost always reinforced at home and is thus the more readily 'internalised', that is, accepted as valid and to a greater or lesser extent incorporated into the values and sense of identity of the person in question. Attempting to imagine the special degree of guilt and shame he accumulated...is, I think, 'the key to understanding Britten's sense of being an outsider'. He rightly adds that we should avoid 'the simplistic claim that here lies the single key to Britten's creative personality'.

Chapter 5
Sussex and Suffolk

According to Peter Pears, Britten was 'very excited and pleased, no question about that' with the success of *Peter Grimes*. Not only had the opera succeeded: its extraordinary impact seemed to mark a revitalisation of British music. Such a revitalisation was needed: a renaissance had begun in the 19th century with Sullivan and Elgar and continued with figures such as Vaughan Williams and Walton, but 'VW' was now elderly and Walton, in his forties, had not sustained his brilliant youthful creativity. Thus Britten was thrilled to find himself needed. With the ending of the war, his pacifism was less contentious, and while there were still mutterings about his private life and unsupported rumours that he owed his success merely to the backing of wealthy patrons, they became more muted. By and large the tide had turned: he saw himself accepted as a major artistic figure and was ready to face his future. As the critic Edward Sackville-West wrote at the time of *Peter Grimes:*

'Much has been written both for and against opera as a form of art, but one thing is certain: no composer who has not mastered music, in all its aspects, can hope to be successful in a medium which involves so strenuous a conjugation of all his musical faculties...A good opera, then, represents the composer at the height of his powers: it must always be a result, never a point of departure (except for future operas). It is a bourne from which the traveller may return, but with an outlook necessarily changed by the experience.'

Thus, arguably, Britten had now found himself both musically and personally – if the distinction is valid – and recognised and welcomed the cultural roots which he had once perhaps wished to set aside. 'I only write while I am at home', he was to say, and that meant his native Suffolk. This Englishness was henceforth to be reflected in several works, not least the many folk song settings that he made for Peter Pears and himself to perform in recitals. Pears later wrote of them:

'They made a very good end to a programme which started with Purcell, went on with Schubert and ended with one of Britten's Cycles. He made something like forty arrangements...The folk-song revival, which started around the turn of the century, was already more or less a thing of the past when Britten was composing in the early thirties, and it had very little effect on his music. He himself found the manifestations of the Movement rather tiresome and certainly could not see himself using folk song as part of the structure of his music. His teacher, Frank Bridge, was not sympathetic to the ideals of the composers taking part and Britten was not encouraged in that direction. It was not therefore to the volumes of the English Folk Song Society that Britten went for his tunes and texts...He found a little, old, charmingly printed book of National Melodies collected by the Victorian composer and teacher, John Hullah. In this book there were some so-called folk-songs which Cecil Sharp [the pioneer collector of these melodies at the beginning of the century] would have thrown out. But Britten took up many of them and 'The Ash Grove' comes from this, so does 'There's none to soothe' and several others.

'His way with a folk-song is very different from that of Cecil Sharp who arranged so many for schools in the first part of the century: one of Sharp's cherished ideals was to bring back to English children those tunes that had been sung to and by their ancestors and he used to arrange these songs for voice and piano with very simple and regularly barred accompaniment. This would not do for Britten. He wanted to recreate these melodies with their texts for concert performances, to make them art-songs, in the tradition of Schubert and even Brahms. He therefore takes the tune as if he had written it himself and thinks himself back into how he would turn it into a song. The result is sometimes artfully simple and almost folk-song-like ('Sally Gardens', 'Waly, Waly', 'The Foggy Dew'), sometimes more elaborate and sophisticated ('The Ash Grove', 'Early one morning'), and still others have an accompaniment of a strong pattern which could reasonably be called Schubertian...'

Thus Britten was not a nationalist composer in the sense understood by Vaughan Williams. Even before him, Bridge, Ireland and Walton had adopted a more cosmopolitan outlook necessary to free English music from provincialism – and, Britten would say, amateurishness. But he did not need to repudiate folk song. Rather, he came to it with affection and made it his own. The procedure had its critics, and while audiences usually liked his folk song arrangements, scholars had reservations, and a typical comment from the 1950s is that of Frank Howes, then the principal music critic of *The Times*,

Henry Purcell (1659-1695).

who noted 'some strained examples' while elsewhere recognising the composer's 'extraordinary mixture of sophisticated ingenuity with simplicity of effect'.

If there was something ambivalent about Britten's attitude to folk song, there was none regarding his great English predecessor Henry Purcell and the tradition of secular and sacred music that he headed. He had discovered him in his student years, and now a fuller knowledge came through performing his songs with Peter Pears. In the late 1940s he began to make 'realisations' of this music, arrangements with the keyboard part filled out from the original figured bass and designed for a modern piano.[1] This was not unlike his technique in the folk song arrangements, where he also proceeded afresh from a given melody. He was to say in an interview in 1961:

'Purcell is a great master at handling the English language in song, and I learned much from him. I recall a critic once asking me from whom I had learned to set English poetry to music. I told him Purcell; he was amazed. I suppose he expected me to say folk music and Vaughan Williams...[my] First Canticle...was certainly modelled on the Purcell *Divine Hymns*; but few people knew their Purcell well enough to realise that.'

Britten's *Canticle 1* is the first of five pieces to which he gave this name, implying an extended song with a sacred text; the last dates from 1974. First performed by Pears and the composer in November 1947, its title is *My Beloved is Mine.* In a symposium on Britten's music published in 1952, Pears was to call it 'Britten's finest piece of vocal music to date...with a classical shape has come repose and dignity.' When the composer, in the interview just quoted, was asked if he agreed at that time, he said, 'Yes, I think so.' In addition, he mentioned his excursions into non-English texts, also relating these to the past: 'I am sure Purcell felt the same way in his own day about this, for surely he was influenced by French and Italian music too.' So, of course, was Bach. In the symposium mentioned above[2], Donald Mitchell was to refute the view of Britten that:

'lying outside nationalist musical considerations he fails to secure a place for himself in our affections...*Britten has created an Englishry of his own*...It seems likely that only a composer who had a whole European heritage behind him could have refreshed the more specifically national sources of his own art with such vitality. Hence the historical importance of Britten's European stylisations – a Europeanism which, as it appears in the new English synthesis of Britten's late music, inevitably makes his Englishry of European validity.'

The timeless East Anglian seascape.

Thus we may argue that Britten's music is English simply in the way that Bach's and Beethoven's are German, and perhaps at heart he did not disagree with Vaughan Williams's dictum, *'Art, like charity, should begin at home'*. For all its eclecticism, *Peter Grimes* is deeply English in its response to the harsher and homelier elements of Crabbe's original poem, to the Suffolk landscape and seascape with its coastal weather, and to the popular institutions of church and pub. A setting of Mattins, off-stage, actually accompanies the crucial scene in Act 2 between Ellen, the apprentice and finally Grimes himself.

Farming, part of the Suffolk way of life.

Britten followed the composition of his opera by writing a short *Festival Te Deum* for a Swindon church. Indeed, though no longer a churchgoer, he was to compose sacred pieces such as this throughout his life. One unsurpassed example from the 1940s is his cantata *Rejoice in the Lamb,* of which Pears told him soon afterwards, 'That is still your best yet you know'. Commissioned in 1943 by the Rev. Walter Hussey for his church, St Matthew's, Northampton, it set an 18th-century text and elicited this praise from Scott Goddard in the Pelican book *British Music in our Time* (1946):

'The delicate, steel-like tension of Christopher Smart's lines is echoed in music that has a similar quality of ageless youth and instinctive unquestioning wisdom. The effect, once it has registered upon the listener, is of music reaching the understanding with a vague, hesitant, yet quite vital touch as from some unexplored region of the mind.'

The religious, English theme continued in a new vocal cycle that Britten now composed for Peter Pears. This was *The Holy Sonnets of John Donne*, first performed by Pears and the composer at the Wigmore Hall on Britten's 32nd birthday, 22 November 1945; on the preceding day, in the same hall, the première had taken place of his *Second String Quartet*, written to commemorate the 250th anniversary of Purcell's death. The history of the *Sonnets'* composition reminds us of the composer's sensitivity to his environment and his ability to turn even illness to creative advantage. Donne's 17th-century texts provide a counterbalance to Michelangelo's in the earlier cycle: where those poems had discussed love, these speak of sin, death and redemption – as would Britten's next opera, *The Rape of Lucretia*. The idea for a Donne cycle was already in the composer's mind when, in the summer of 1945, he went with the violinist Yehudi Menuhin on a recital tour of German concentration camps, where many liberated prisoners remained because they were as yet too ill to return to their homes. On returning to England, he fell ill and wrote the nine songs, as he later said, 'in a week while in bed with a high fever, a delayed reaction from an inoculation'. He added that this tour had been 'in many ways a terrifying experience. The theme of the *Donne Sonnets* is death, as you know. I think the connection between personal experience and my feelings about the poetry was a strong one. It certainly characterised the music.'

The last song in this cycle, called 'Death, be not proud', is a Purcellian passacaglia (i.e., the music is unified by a 'ground

The producer, Eric Crozier.

bass', a phrase in a strong B major tonality that is repeated throughout under the vocal line and changing piano harmony. Pears later wrote of this music written in response to the horrors of Belsen: 'Death has been conquered, not by an old man who waits for it resigned and patient, but on the contrary by a still young one who defies the nightmare horror with a strong love, the instinctive answer to Buchenwald from East Anglia.'

The success of *Peter Grimes* had aroused much curiosity and speculation as to what opera Britten might write next. In fact, he was to compose three more within the next four years. Yet not one was a 'grand opera' with a big orchestra and chorus, as *Grimes* had been, and the reason was only partly artistic. The bickering surrounding *Grimes* at Sadler's Wells had focused largely on Joan Cross, whom the company's governors, under pressure from some singers, eventually asked to resign. After her departure, Peter Pears and Eric Crozier soon followed. Thus, where were new Britten operas to be produced? Fortunately, Glyndebourne, the private opera house of the wealthy auctioneer John Christie, came to the rescue. Seating 600 people, this Sussex theatre had been closed during the war but was due to reopen in 1946, and for this occasion Christie agreed to mount a new Britten opera. This was *The Rape of Lucretia*, a chamber opera with eight singers and an orchestra of just 12 players.

Some time earlier, Eric Crozier, with experience in the French theatre, had lent Britten a copy of André Obey's play *Le viol de Lucrèce*. Britten invited Ronald Duncan, a pre-war collaborator, to write the libretto, which also drew on Shakespeare's poem on the same subject, while Crozier agreed to produce. The painter and designer John Piper, another fomer colleague, was also Britten's choice. Later the composer was to insist on his involvement at every stage of the creation of a new opera, saying, 'I have to be in on it from the beginning', and that all concerned should work in the closest contact, from the most preliminary stages right up to the first night. For *The Rape of Lucretia*, two casts and two conductors were selected, since 14 performances were to be given within a two-week period.

Kathleen Ferrier in the role of Lucretia.

One of the Lucretias was Kathleen Ferrier, well known as a concert singer but with little stage experience. Ronald Duncan later described her audition for Britten and himself:

'She was so terrified she could only whisper. We wondered how she could possibly sing...He cut the talk to a minimum and handed her the score. She read it through once, then went to the piano and sang part of the Spinning Aria. We were both so moved by the quality of her voice that neither of us spoke. I had been impressed, too, by the genuine feeling of purity which came over. This was a very necessary quality for the part...We had been extremely lucky. She was not only vocally perfect but it could not have been better casting from my point of view.'

A rehearsal for *The Rape of Lucretia* at Glyndeboume. The composer plays the piano, Emest Ansermet stands to the right of the piano, Nancy Evans stands centre, Ronald Duncan stands far left, Aksel Schiøtz stands back left and Flora Nielsen stands right of centre.

The other Lucretia was Eric Crozier's wife-to-be Nancy Evans, while Peter Pears and Joan Cross (doubling with Aksel Schiøtz and Flora Nielsen) were the Male and Female Chorus who, from stage left and right, provide a Christian commentary on the quasi-historical but pre-Christian story. The conductors were Ernest Ansermet and Reginald Goodall. According to Duncan, the final preparations for *The Rape of Lucretia* were tense:

'Everybody became very nervous as we approached the first night of the opera at Glyndebourne; so much depended on it. It was the first new opera to be presented there. Kathleen Ferrier had some reason to be nervous: it was her first appearance on a stage. A feud had arisen between the producer, Eric Crozier, and Rudolf Bing, the Glyndebourne manager. Ben himself was making Christie a target for all his nervous tension. The peace was only kept by the extraordinary tact of two people, Audrey Christie and Ernest Ansermet. The night before the first performance [on 12 July 1946] I dreamed that Christie had told us all to leave Glyndebourne.'

The Rape of Lucretia disappointed some people simply by being different from *Peter Grimes* – though a big opera with mass effects could not have been considered for Glyndebourne's small stage and auditorium.[3] Another complaint concerned the Christian viewpoint with which the Roman story was presented, which, according to *The Times*, constituted a 'grave dramatic error'. Yet Stravinsky's opera-oratorio *Oedipus rex* has a similarly anachronistic commentary by a narrator in modern dress. Duncan's self-consciously literary libretto also drew fire; some lines, subsequently expunged, ran, 'The oatmeal slippers of sleep / Creep through the city and drag / The sable shadows of night / Over the limbs of light', and even the sympathetic Edward Sackville-West wrote of 'inappropriate jokes, absurd anachronisms'. Still, the music was admired, Frank Howes finding 'a very sure touch...the age-old balance of music and drama is struck anew' and Scott Goddard in the *News Chronicle* saluting 'a masterly work'. However, only Ferruccio Bonavia, writing in the *New York Times*, called the new opera an advance on *Peter Grimes*, finding more beauty, range and a 'deepening of sympathy'.

Britten may have expected the fullest understanding from his fellow composer Michael Tippett. But Tippett's later memory of this production suggests his insensitivity and helps us to comprehend why the two men never attained a comfortable relationship. After seeing it he went backstage and confronted Britten:

'I said: 'Oh dear!' He said: 'What do you mean by "Oh dear"?' I may have said: 'I think it's more interesting than *Grimes*' – I'm not sure what I said. But I did say: 'If you're now going to write a comic opera' – as he'd already told me – 'for Christ's sake don't use this librettist.' Ben took it, but he withdrew. He was already in a touchy state.'

On the other hand, Britten responded warmly to a letter from Imogen Holst:

'Your understanding of my work, of Lucretia especially, gives me great encouragement. Especially the manner in which you approach the Christian idea delighted me. I used to think that the day when one could shock people was over – but now, I've discovered that being simple and considering things spiritual of importance, produces violent reactions!'

As for Britten's projected comic opera, also intended for Glyndebourne in the following year, it nearly did not materialise, for *Lucretia* then toured to poor houses in Edinburgh, Glasgow, Liverpool, Manchester and Oxford and as its financial guarantor, John Christie lost something like £14,000. That might have ended Glyndebourne's support of his work, had Christie not already advertised the return of the 'Glyndebourne English Opera Company' with 'a new Contemporary Opera' for 1947, the comedy *Albert Herring*.

In the meantime, Britten flew to America, where *Peter Grimes* was being staged at Koussevitzsky's Berkshire Festival at Tanglewood, Massachusetts. The conductor was the 27-year-old Leonard Bernstein, a Koussevitzsky pupil and now his assistant, who had already met Britten in England and seen *The Rape of Lucretia*. It must have been pleasant for the composer to revisit the USA as a fêted figure, and Wystan Auden made a point of getting to Tanglewood to see the production. However, their reunion was hardly a success: Britten disliked having to share a room with him (a heavy smoker, Auden even smoked in bed) and hear him call the performance 'terrible'. Eric Crozier, who produced, had tried to discourage the composer from attending (in overfed America, he could not find a boy who looked like a half-starved apprentice), but whatever Britten's private views of the production, he called it 'a lively student performance'. To Bernstein, he appeared 'slightly mistrustful, very shy, but when he had a point to make...there was no question about it.' As for Auden, according to Peter Pears, 'Ben was on a different track now, and he was no longer prepared to be dominated – bullied – by Wystan.'

On returning to Britain, Britten quickly composed a busy *Occasional Overture* (i.e. an overture to mark an occasion) for the concert opening the BBC Third Programme on 29 September 1946, but became dissatisfied with it and withdrew it after the performance to join *Young Apollo* and *Paul Bunyan* in limbo. (Today, however, all three works have been performed and are available on record.) However, another commissioned work, first heard that October, at once hit its target. This was *The Young Person's Guide to the Orchestra*, a set of variations on a theme by Purcell that featured the orchestral instruments in turn, not least in the brilliant final fugue. Written for the Crown Film Unit, it immediately took on a life of its own in the concert hall, and indeed, the first concert performance was given before the release of the film. Dedicated to the children of his friends John and Jean Maud 'for their edification and entertainment', the exuberant and uncomplicated *Young Person's Guide* has become Britten's most popular orchestral work.

Now in his early thirties, Britten was continuously in demand, though this enviable position had drawbacks and he constantly had to prioritise his work. He conducted performances of his music, joined Pears in recital tours that now took in the western European countries, and gave thought to his new comic opera for Glyndebourne. It was he and his associates – Pears, Cross, Crozier and Piper – who created the new company that was to present the new opera and take it on tour. Named the English Opera Group, and requiring around £12,000 for its launch, it was a considerable venture. Contracts had to be offered to singers, orchestral players and stage staff, and some sort of administrative structure set up. A prospectus dating from early 1947, backed by a board of management that included Ralph Hawkes, Tyrone Guthrie and Sir Kenneth (later Lord) Clark, ran as follows:

'We believe the time has come when England, which has never had a tradition of native opera, but has always depended upon a repertory of foreign works, can create its own operas. Opera is as much a vital means of artistic expression as orchestral music, drama and painting. The lack of it has meant a certain impoverishment of English artistic life. We believe the best way to achieve the beginnings of a repertory of English operas is through the creation of a form of opera requiring small resources of singers and players, but suitable for performance in large or small opera houses or theatres. A first essay in this direction was the writing and staging of Britten's *The Rape of Lucretia* in 1946...The success of this experiment has encouraged the three persons chiefly involved [the artistic directors Britten, Crozier and Piper]...to continue their work as a group by establishing, under their artistic direction, a new opera company to be known as *THE ENGLISH OPERA GROUP*, incorporated on a non-profit-making basis. This Group will give annual seasons of contemporary opera in English and suitable classical works including those of Purcell. It is part of the Group's purpose to encourage young composers to write for the operatic stage, also to encourage poets and playwrights to tackle the problem of writing libretti in collaboration with composers.'

63

This prospectus also stated that the support of leading performers was assured, and appealed for funds of the order of £10,000 to supplement money already promised (£2,000) by the composer's wealthy friends Leonard and Dorothy Elmhirst of Dartington Hall [4] It went on to say that 'Benjamin Britten is now writing his third opera – *Albert Herring*, a comedy about life in a Suffolk village [which] will open at Glyndebourne on June 20th.'

For the libretto of this third opera, Britten turned again to a new writer. This time it was Eric Crozier, who knew Suffolk well and, as a producer, had proved a gifted collaborator, quicker-minded than Montagu Slater and free from Ronald Duncan's literary pretentiousness. The composer consulted him as to a choice of story, and Crozier writes:

'I suggested a comic opera based on Maupassant's short story *Le Rosier de Madame Husson*. Britten liked the idea, especially when he saw how easily the action could be transplanted from Maupassant's France to his own native coast of East Suffolk. We made a brief sketch of how the story might be adapted as an opera, and, before I quite understood what was happening, it was agreed that I should undertake the libretto.'

Like *Lucretia*, *Albert Herring* used a small group of solo singers (and no chorus) plus a 12-piece orchestra. But here the similarity ends. The atmospheres of the two operas could not be more different, with *Lucretia*'s powerful Roman drama giving place to a sunny English-provincial comedy. Since Eric Crozier's grandfather had had a country shop in Suffolk, where as a boy he had helped behind the counter, Mrs Herring's greengrocery in the little market town of Loxford seems highly authentic; there is also a place called Yoxford and the outlying villages mentioned in his libretto (Ufford, Orford, Iken, Snape and Campsey Ash) actually exist. Furthermore, the names of several characters had living antecedents: Albert Herring was a Tunstall grocer, Nancy the baker's daughter was named after Nancy Evans who created the role, Florence the housekeeper was called after Joan Cross's own housekeeper, the vicar Mr Gedge took his name from a London clergyman, the name of the boy Harold Wood is that of a local railway station, and Cissie Woodger was a Suffolk girl to whom Britten once gave a concert ticket (asked next day how she had enjoyed herself, she replied, 'Oh, I didn't mind it at all!').

A scene from *Albert Herring*; Joan Cross as formidable Lady Billows, Gladys Parr as Florence and Roy Ashton as the mayor.

Albert Herring tells of an amiable youth tied to his widowed mother's apron strings and serving in her shop. Lady Billows and her committee of local worthies fail to find a suitably chaste village girl to be May Queen, their choice lights on him, and under protest and to the amusement of his contemporaries and the local children, he is duly elected and crowned at a village feast – before which Sid and Nancy, a pair of young lovers, secretly lace his lemonade with rum. Returning home before his mother, and tipsy for the first time in his life, Albert hears the lovers flirting outside his window and realises how much he is missing in life. He plucks up courage and, fingering the 25 sovereigns he has received as a prize for virtue, goes off on a nocturnal spree. In the final act of the opera, next day, everyone is anxiously searching for him, and when his festal wreath of orange-blossom is found on a road, crushed, all presume his death and, united by grief, sing a moving threnody. At this point Albert returns, dishevelled but proud. At once grief turns to fury as all turn on him with reproaches, but he politely dismisses them from his shop and firmly puts his mother in her place. As Sid, Nancy and the children delightedly

A scene from *Albert Herring*. Pears in the title role, overhears Sid and Nancy (Frederick Sharp and Nancy Evans) sing a love duet.

celebrate his new freedom with him, he skims his wreath out over the audience as the curtain falls.

Considering the life-enhancing nature of this splendid comedy, which like all great comedies also makes a serious statement about the whole human condition, it is unfortunate that the occasional commentator sees it chiefly as a sexual parable – something which, according to Crozier, was never intended. Thus in 1994, in an 'international journal of gay and lesbian studies', Clifford Hindley writes, '*Albert Herring* is the study of a young homosexual who breaks free of his inhibitions'; however, Mr Hindley also finds homosexual elements in six further Britten operas including *Peter Grimes*, and thinks it 'very likely that further study would reveal homosexual resonances' in yet others besides these. Without going so far, it is fair to link Britten's own personal development to Albert's renunciation of his mother's tyranny and his essentially negative 'virtue'. As this opera demonstrates, he had won his way through to a new confidence and vitality, and its mastery shows him at the height of his youthful powers.

Though *Albert Herring* was an immediate success, John Christie snobbishly disliked this opera set in a shop and told people, 'This isn't *our* kind of thing, you know', and *The Times* thought it 'a charade'. That review nearly sank an engagement with the Holland Festival, but in the event Dutch audiences liked the opera and Britten told his friends the Mauds, 'Albert was much to their taste (even to the critics' taste!!).' Leaving

Holland in August 1947, the English Opera Group set off for Lucerne in Switzerland, where they were to perform both *Herring* and *Lucretia*.

While the company's scenery travelled in three lorries and most of the cast went by train, Britten, Pears, Crozier and Nancy Evans drove south in the composer's old Rolls-Royce tourer, whose hood could be lowered for their enjoyment of the fresh air and sunshine. However, during the journey they faced the fact that, despite the English Opera Group's artistic success and its receipt of support from the British Council, their European tour would still make a loss: it was simply impractical to carry forty people and scenery around Europe for just a dozen performances. Pears then asked, one evening over pre-dinner drinks:

'Why not make our own Festival? A modest Festival with a few concerts given by friends? Why do we have to come abroad to Switzerland to perform *Albert Herring*? Why can't we perform it at Aldeburgh?'

The town of Aldeburgh was now Britten's home. Having sold his Old Mill at Snape, he had, that June, bought a house on the Aldeburgh sea front called Crag House – later the name became 4 Crabbe Street – and he was shortly to move in. Could he and his colleagues mount a Festival in this remote Suffolk town to which people would come, given that its road and rail links with London were poor, and that it was a place where, at least in Crabbe's time, locals might 'scowl at strangers with suspicious eye'? Would the local golfing and sailing gentry – retired company chairmen and senior officers – support concerts and opera, particularly where 'modern music' was concerned? Would the ordinary townsfolk give their support? Was Aldeburgh's Jubilee Hall big enough to accommodate operatic performances? Everything was discussed as thoroughly as possible.

Finally, the planners agreed that, if the Jubilee Hall was viable for the staging of small-scale opera, they would try to mount a Festival in 1948. On returning to England, they hurried to Aldeburgh, talked to the mayor, the vicar and the Countess of Cranbrook, a young mother and music-lover who accepted the chairmanship of an executive committee. In January 1948, a public meeting took place to discuss the venture, and when funds were promised from various sources including the founders themselves, it became clear that a week-long programme could be planned for June. A manager was appointed and set up an office in the Wentworth Hotel. Imogen Holst has described these preparations, not dissimilar from the May Day plans in *Herring*'s Loxford:

'Members of the local amateur dramatic society and the Women's Institure spent day after day addressing envelopes for the advance publicity; in the late spring fresh coats of paint appeared on many of the houses, and by the time it was June and the audiences began to arrive, the houses and shops in the High Street had their window-ledges and balconies decorated with armfuls of flowers, including the beautiful yellow tree-lupins that still grow in profusion at the edge of the marshes.'

To everyone's satisfaction, this town which E.M. Forster had called a 'bleak little place; not beautiful' prepared wholeheartedly to welcome strangers. Forster himself was invited to give a Festival lecture on Crabbe and *Grimes* and found the Baptist Chapel 'painted up in cream and chocolate'. William Plomer, the future librettist of Britten's opera *Gloriana* and his three church parables, also came and lectured on Edward FitzGerald, who was, like Crabbe, a Suffolk man. Musically, the Festival opened on 5 June with a Parish Church concert whose chief item was Britten's new cantata *Saint Nicolas*, to a Crozier text. Nicolas

Britten conducts a performance of *St Nicolas* in Lancing College Chapel, July 1948. Peter Pears is seen to his right, as soloist.

was a patron saint of Peter Pears's old school, Lancing College in Sussex, and the work had been commissioned to mark its centenary. A performance there was to take place on 24 July, but in the meantime the school conceded the première to Aldeburgh. It involved local children's choirs as well as professionals (Pears was the soloist representing Nicolas himself), and made a profound impression. For Forster, 'the sudden contrast between elaborate singing and the rough breathy voices of three kids from a local "Co-op" made one swallow in the throat and water in the eyes. It was one of those triumphs outside the rules of art which only a great artist can achieve.' Donald Mitchell wrote: 'I was so confused by its progressively overwhelming impact that all I could find to say was: "This is too beautiful".'

Saint Nicolas is in nine sections and tells the story of the fourth-century saint in dramatic, almost operatic music. There is a charming and innocent waltz to depict his birth and boyhood and a thrilling choral storm at sea, together with two English hymns in which the audience/congregation joins and a plainchant Nunc Dimittis as he dies. His death is presented positively, as he sings, *'Lord, I come to life, to final birth'*, and the final hymn that follows, *'God moves in a mysterious way'*, is deeply affirmative. In this same 1948 Aldeburgh Festival, Forster attended the opening *Albert Herring* performance in the Jubilee Hall, where on the little stage the children's ball game in Act 1 had to be played carefully, and wrote:

'It was delightful to burst out in the intervals on to the beach, or to watch the crowd who were partly in evening dress and partly dressed anyhow, and exempt from the drilled smartness of Glyndebourne. During the first interval a man in a pub said: "I took a ticket for this show because it is local and I felt I had to...I wouldn't part with it now for ten pounds".'

Thus Britten had now put down roots, living and working in a town close to his birthplace and facing the same North Sea: indeed, as *Albert Herring* proved, East Suffolk could even inspire an opera with international appeal. His friendship and collaboration with Peter Pears promised an equal permanence. His life was taking on its future pattern, that of a working composer in the kind of community that had given him his upbringing, and, indeed, he was to declare, 'I want to serve the community'. Furthermore, *Saint Nicolas* seems like an affirmation of the Anglican faith of his childhood. Can one say of Britten, as Auden's biographer Charles Osborne writes of the poet, that he found in his thirties that 'the faith drilled into him as a child had by no means died'? Perhaps, for Eric Walter White wrote in a biography which he authorised, 'His religious beliefs are central to his life and his work.' [5] Though Britten was not a regular churchgoer, his priest friend Walter Hussey said that he 'believed wholeheartedly in a power greater than the universe' and even declared, 'I am coming to feel more and more that all my music must be written to the glory of God.' Among his later works, *Noye's Fludde*, the *War Requiem* and the three church parables all embody a spiritual statement, and of the *War Requiem* he said, 'the message is what counts'.

[1] The figured bass of baroque accompaniments, also sometimes called *continuo,* consisted merely of the actual bass notes and an indication of the harmony expressed in numbers. The exact notes were left to the performer.

[2] *Benjamin Britten: a Commentary on his work from a group of specialists,* edited by Donald Mitchell and Hans Keller (London, 1952) is an important pioneering book but made claims for the composer that upset some people. One such was Hans Keller's 'for the first time Mozart, the universal musician who masters everything with a somnambulistic surefootedness and grace, has found a companion'. Predictably, there was a sharp reaction, and in the *Sunday Times* Ernest Newman described this symposium as 'frankly of the adoring order'. Much later, in 1991, Mitchell was to say: 'Now, of course, the tone of the whole thing makes me cringe a bit. But I certainly don't disown it; nor would Hans have done…I'm not at all apologetic in claiming for the book a certain historical importance. Its critics of course tried to rubbish it. But who remembers them now?'.

[3] In 1994, *Grimes* was to be given there for the first time, following rebuilding and enlargement.

[4] Dartington, near Totnes in Devon, was a fine old house in large grounds. Its owners the Elmhirsts supported the arts and it had an Arts Centre at which Imogen Holst directed the music. In 1944, Dartington proposed the idea of a teaching music festival for

some 100 resident students which Britten would direct. Although this did not materialise, he and Pears made several professional visits and in July 1945, with Joan Cross, they performed excerpts from *Peter Grimes*. An annual Summer School of music has taken place there since 1953.

[5] White's book, *Benjamin Britten: His Life and Operas* (London 1970), has since appeared in a second edition edited by John Evans (Faber and Faber 1983).

Chapter 6

Salvation at Sea

Britten with his dachshund, Gilda.

Eric Walter White, Britten's first biographer, considered that he reached complete maturity in his early thirties and that by 1948 'the full extent of his remarkable gifts had been revealed – the fluency, the protean variety, the feeling for effect, the love of setting words to music, and the deceptive simplicity of the melodic and harmonic means employed.' By fluency, White evidently meant Britten's workmanlike attitude to composing, writing to order and keeping to a schedule. 'I believe strongly in a routine', he was to say in 1961. Much planning went on in his head, often during afternoon walks with his dog (he had several dachshunds over the years): whether composition went well, or not, he could sit working at his desk throughout the morning and again in the late afternoon and early evening. Imogen Holst, who assisted him when he wrote his opera *Gloriana* in 1953, described his speed in orchestration on the large pages of manuscript paper that she prepared for him, doing tasks like ruling barlines and putting in instrument names: 'I was dismayed to see how quickly he wrote – he could get through 28 pages in a day. I thought I should

Britten at work in The Red House in the late 1950s.

never catch up with him...He seldom had to stop and think.' Such was his concentration and determination that she also recalled 'one pouring wet day when he got soaked through while sitting indoors at his desk because he hadn't noticed that the rain was coming in on him.' Such intense mental activity inevitably took its toll and he could be weary and sad. 'Did your father [the composer] *always* enjoy working?', he asked her, and, after finishing one big orchestral score, he wrote, 'Thank God it is over and done with (all except those.......metronome-marks [1])' – the dots are his own and probably stand for 'bloody', a word he sometimes used.

Indeed, like his protagonist Aschenbach in his last opera, *Death in Venice*, Britten was 'driven on' by the creative process, and the satisfaction he felt on completing a new piece was usually short-lived. Though his large catalogue of works does indeed demonstrate fluency, this was due less to facility than to his craftsman's discipline and professionalism, and in a 1961 interview he was to say bluntly, 'Composition is never easy.' Yet he admitted to becoming 'excited about work in hand', adding,

'Often I get exceedingly impatient if I am prevented from completing a work. If I have to leave Aldeburgh and an incomplete work, I am often ill because I fret so much. My state of mind is reflected in my body.'

The composer conducting a recording of *St Nicolas* in April 1955 at Aldeburgh Parish Church.

This situation in turn created friction between him and Pears: they were now in constant demand as a performing duo, but touring with his partner (as Pears understandably wanted him to do) interrupted the composition which he always saw as his main vocation. Yet he also needed Pears and could resent the periods of separation caused by the singer's pursuit of his own busy career. Indeed, Pears had never fully settled at Aldeburgh, acquiring in 1946 his own London house, where his elderly parents also lived (as did Britten when in town), though he sold it in 1948 after their deaths.[2] In a letter of that year, Britten apologised to a woman friend who had stayed with them at Aldeburgh and 'got muddled up in a bit of a purely domestic tiff...it was really all my fault for being touchy and silly – caused largely by my tummy & general pregnancy [with a new work, the *Spring Symphony*]...I do hope it didn't leave a nasty taste in your mouth...' When he and Pears then set off to give recitals in Holland, his stomach 'went *all* wrong again...I had to cancel one concert & only staggered thro' the others.' Back in Aldeburgh, he was diagnosed as suffering from nervous exhaustion and advised to rest for three months, calling himself 'grumpy & nervy, & incapable of thought!' As for Pears, 'Peter is hard breadwinning...but gets here occasionally'. He told Pears in a letter that December:

'I *do* adore working with you, & think we really achieve something together. My only way of coming sane thro' this miserable time is to think that this [resting under doctor's orders] will make it possible for us to continue working together in the future, & if I *didn't* rest we might have had to cut it out altogether.'

Clearly worried, Pears took Britten off to Italy in January 1949, whence, in a characteristic mood-swing, Britten told his sister Barbara of 'perfect sun & weather...& we're both feeling on top of the world!'. Yet on returning, he fell back into depression, writing to Pears on 19 February, 'I am sorry I was so gloomy yesterday, but it was the bottom of the well for me. Work was impossible, & I felt absolutely desperate'.

Inevitably, such mood-swings tested Pears's patience, and Britten once told his lifelong friend Marion Stein, 'Peter gets cross when I'm ill'[(3)] Yet that single remark falls far short of the whole story, and their relationship cannot be summed up so simply, although Britten's variable health and state of mind was always part of it. Much later, in 1962, Pears was to tell him in a letter, with patent sincerity:

'Your letter simply makes me go hot with shame – That *you* should be asking me to forgive you for being ill, when it is I that should be looking after you & loving you, should long ago have thrown my silly career out of the window & come and tried to protect you a bit from worry and tension, instead of adding to them with my own worries and tetchinesses!'

Even so, Pears knew that Britten's illnesses and tensions, real and distressing though they were, could fire his creative processes – as happened with the *Donne Sonnets* – and that his friend could never have felt, or wished to feel, like Richard Strauss, who said of his *Alpine Symphony* that he wanted 'to compose as a cow gives milk'. As for Britten, to know what Pears meant to him and put all this in perspective, we only need to read what he told him in 1966, as he convalesced after an operation for diverticulitis:

'It may not seem like it to you, but what you think or feel is really the most important thing in my life. It is an unbelievable thing to be spending my life with you: I can't think what the Gods were doing to allow it to happen! You have been so wonderful to me, given me so much of your life, such wonderful experiences, knowledge & wisdom which I never could have approached without you. And above all – your love.'

Britten never rested on his laurels, and did not consider himself a *'great musician'* of the order of Mozart, Bach or Schubert. When the Mitchell-Keller symposium came out in 1952, he merely remarked, 'I've come to the conclusion that I must have a very clever subconscious', and as late as 1968 he was still able to tell Imogen Holst, 'one day I'll be able to relax a bit, and try and become a good composer.' He took small pleasure in the praise of scholars, and Peter Pears told me that he resented their earnest analysis of his music as 'a kind of prying'. The pianist Graham Johnson, who as a young man knew Britten in his last years, found him 'very disinclined to be analytical for the purposes of savouring the triumphs of his achievements. I was intensely interested, and I think he found this rather wearing. It was as if there was a special secret about composition and creative flow which would somehow be spoiled by analysing it too much.'

Though sympathetic with amateurs, whose music-making he found 'fresh and unstrained', Britten maintained rigorous professional standards, and collaborators failing to come up to the mark were dropped. Sometimes this was done in a kindly way, but not always, and if people have called him ruthless, they have done so with some justice. He sharply condemned 'the ineptitude of some professionals who don't know their stuff – I have no patience with that,' and once declared, 'I have recently heard several performances of my own pieces and I felt so depressed that I considered chucking it all up! Wrong tempi, stupid phrasing and poor technique – in fact non-sense.'

Sometimes Britten turned his irritation on his friends. Walter Hussey, preaching at the 1953 Aldeburgh Festival, remembered later how Wystan Auden had been there as a guest lecturer. Britten probably regretted this invitation issued some time previously, since Auden had adversely criticised his opera *Gloriana* earlier that summer. [4] 'Big and overwhelming', said Hussey, Auden expected to be the centre of attraction and unchanged in his habit of laying down the law, but on Britten's home ground, which he dubbed 'Addleborough' and considered

The composer with his sister Barbara and Lord Harewood at a Festival fundraising fete in 1955.

to typify the composer's timid provincialism, he was kept at a distance. 'I was never allowed to see Ben alone', he told Elizabeth: 'I feared as much, still, I was a bit sad'. Humphrey Carpenter, the biographer of both men, writes that 'after their 1953 meeting at Aldeburgh, Britten would have nothing further to do with Auden'. (Twenty years later, however, he wept on hearing of the poet's death.)

Even after Auden's departure from that Festival, Britten still smouldered. Walter Hussey gave his sermon at a morning service during which Lord Harewood read the lesson on the parable of the talents, and he returned to Britten's house for lunch, the other guests being the Harewoods, the French cultural attaché and his wife, and Barbara Britten:

'They had a long dining room, and a huge long refectory table, quite narrow, with benches on either side. Ben was giving a recital in the afternoon, with the Amadeus Quartet: I think he was playing the Schubert 'Trout' Quintet. And Peter came in before lunch and said, 'Ben won't be in to lunch, if you wouldn't mind carrying on on your own. He's just a bit worried. But if he *does* come, take no notice at all – but I'm sure he won't.' So we all sat down to lunch – I think it was a cold lunch. We all were at one end of the table, so that there was a huge empty space up at the other end. Peter wasn't there. And we were having a discussion on the parable of the talents: Harewood was talking very intelligently. Suddenly the door opened and in came Ben, looking like death – like he could, you know. He looked simply awful: drawn and droopy and everything. And he never said a word. Of course, all conversation stopped dead. Then together we all went on, as if nothing had happened. Ben sat down, on the same side as I, but right on the far end, leaving an enormous gap. And we went on busily discussing the talents and almost forgot him. Then suddenly we were interrupted by a hysterical voice from the other end of the table: 'It's those who have no talents at all – they're the real problem!' And of course we were absolutely silenced. You couldn't really say anything. Then – fools rushing in where angels fear to tread – I said, 'Meaning yourself, Ben?' And he said in the same hysterical voice, 'There are times when I feel I have no talents – no talents at all!' And so, again, a great silence. Then I leant forward and said, 'You know, Ben, when you're in this sort of mood we love you best of all.' And he simply gave a great shout. 'I hate you, Walter!' From that moment, he was entirely all right! It was very strange: a tremendous tension built up, and then it was like lancing a boil. After that he chatted and was friendly and went off and gave a marvellous concert.'

Britten once remarked wryly that his doctor had told him he was neurotic. According to the *Concise Oxford Dictionary,* the word can mean two things, 'affected with nervous disorder' or simply 'of abnormal sensibility'. The latter definition sounds less unhealthy if we substitute 'exceptional' for 'abnormal'. An artist is almost by definition exceptional, and Stravinsky, using curious Americanese, called a genius a 'hopeful monster' – someone unusual but in a positive sense. Britten enlarged on this theme when he received the Freedom of the Borough of Lowestoft in 1951, saying that, while composers belonged to the same species as 'ordinary' people, their thought and feeling had to go deeper. 'Artists are artists', he declared,

'because they have an extra sensitivity – a skin less, perhaps than other people...[so] when you hear of an artist saying or doing something strange or unpopular, think of that extra sensitivity – that skin less...It is a proud privilege to be a creative artist, but it can also be painful.'

Since Britten's death, some commentators have argued that his lifelong touchiness was due to conflicts arising from his sexuality. He himself disliked being labelled in any way, and would have hated such attempts to 'explain' his work and personality. Beth Welford considered her brother to be simply 'a very private person who believed in decent living', and Peter Pears emphatically denied to me that he was burdened by guilt in a way that some (even among his admirers) might like to suppose. 'Forget it!', he told another biographer, Michael Kennedy. However, the conductor Norman Del Mar,[4] who knew Britten well in the 1950s, says, 'Of course Peter would say that...Ben really was tortured by homosexuality', while Ronald Duncan called the composer 'a man in flight from himself', and for Leonard Bernstein, himself bisexual, he was 'at odds with the world'. But we may let Pears have the last word here. 'Ben never regarded his passionate feelings for me or his earlier friends as anything but good, natural, and profoundly creative. In that direction there was never a moment of guilt...Is one really interested in the sex life of the great musicians or the less great?' In a letter written just after Britten's death, he declared, 'He was a *good* man. How could he not be having written all that beautiful music?'

On the whole, this private man also refrained from waving banners in the service of causes, and making *ex cathedra* pronouncements about music. Though such avoidance seems negative in a media-conscious society, it provided an interesting and revealing theme for his speech accepting an honorary music doctorate at Hull University in 1962. 'I am a creative artist and therefore suffer frequently from depressions and lack of confidence', he said, and went on:

'I admit that I hate speaking in public. It is not really a matter of natural shyness, but because I do not easily think in words, because words are not my medium. This may surprise some people, but I suppose it is the way one's brain is made. I have always found reading music easier than reading books...I also have a very real dread of becoming one of those artists who *talk*. I believe so strongly that it is dangerous for artists to *talk* – in public, that is; in private one really cannot stop them! – the artist's job is to *do*, not to talkabout what he does. *That* is the job of other people (critics, for instance but I'm not always so sure about this). I am all for listening to music, looking at pictures, reading novels – rather than talking about them. It is natural for composers to have strong opinions about music, and very narrow ones. They have to be selective...Of course I have said silly things – and these were eagerly taken up in some quarters. This sort of thing, provocative and rather scandalous, always is taken up, because it makes news...one particular composer I can think of, one of the greatest artistic figures of our time [probably Stravinsky] has said some very misleading things, things which must have bewildered many young compsers, many musical people. His judgements of other men's music often seem to me arrogant and ignorant, and they are always changing...how I wish he would keep quiet about them...We should try to be obliging if we are asked to speak in public, but keep off our own personal likes and dislikes.'

From the first Aldeburgh Festival onwards, each Festival had to have one or more new Britten compositions. 1949 brought another Crozier collaboration, the children's opera *The Little Sweep* that was contained in an 'entertainment' called *Let's make an Opera*. Britten's idea for such a piece went back at least to 1940, when he had written in a *New York Times* article of 'school operas...and pieces for the numberless school children learning to play instruments'. As he and his librettist discussed possible stories, it was the composer who hit on the right one. Having in childhood played the sweep-boy Tom in Kingsley's *The Water Babies*, he now remembered that role (coincidentally, Tom's cruel master is named Grimes) and also the child sweep-boy in Blake's *Songs of Innocence*, sold into servitude by his widowed father. During that evening, he and Crozier planned their characters and scenario (one remembers his demand for involvement in drama and staging from the start), and the music was written in two weeks in April. In this short and lively opera, the eight-year-old Sammy, sent to sweep the chimneys of Iken Hall in Suffolk, is rescued from a life of drudgery by a kindly nurserymaid and three children. One successful feature was the use of the audience for four songs. At the première in the Jubilee Hall that June, some people raised their eyebrows at the five-four time signature and dissonant diminished octaves of the opening 'Sweep's Song' – though not the Ipswich schoolchildren taking part, who sang with confidence and skill.

Another new work, unconnected with Aldeburgh, was a choral *Spring Symphony,* commissioned by Koussevitzsky for the Boston Symphony Orchestra. Peter Pears and Kathleen Ferrier were soloists at its first performance in July 1949, during the Holland Festival, Koussevitzsky conducted the American première on 13 August, and finally a British audience heard it first in March 1950. Like *The Little Sweep,* this choral symphony offers a vivid portrait of childhood, although that is only part of the picture, using a boys' choir in the section called 'The Driving Boy', with its image of 'school-boys playing in the stream', and the triumphant statement of the 13th-century song 'Sumer is icumen in' near the end. As with *Albert Herring*, here were happy endings, and the anguish that we meet in the *Sinfonia da Requiem* and *Peter Grimes* might seem to have been banished from Britten's music.

That was not so, but he could now cope better with tough subjects. In 1949, another big operatic project on a harrowing tale (that of Melville's doomed sailor Billy Budd) was already getting under way, but it did not frighten him, and a letter of 15 March 1949 to his friends the Mauds shows him in buoyant mood:

'Work is going magnificently. The opera libretto with Morgan Forster is ploughing ahead, & I feel it is going to be a very big thing indeed...[it's] heavenly weather today...what fun the opera work is being, & how pleased I am to have got the old symphony polished off!'

E. M. Forster working on the libretto for *Billy Budd* at Crag House, with Eric Crozier.

Despite this optimism, *Billy Budd* was to bring him headaches and heartaches. Commissioned by the Arts Council for the 1951 Festival of Britain, this was a grand opera for Covent Garden and on the scale of *Peter Grimes*. Here, too, the protagonist is persecuted and killed, but Budd is no outsider but the handsome and innocent young sailor of Herman

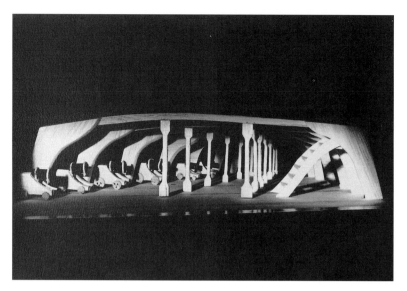

The set model for the opera *Billy Budd*.

Melville's novella, liked by all save his ship's cruel master-at-arms, Claggart, whose hatred of beauty and goodness makes him seek Billy's death. This time, E.M. Forster was Britten's choice of librettist, a writer whom Britten admired and who had become a friend; he had also lectured on Melville's story at Cambridge. However, he was now 70 and had no stage experience, and after their first discussions the composer also invited Eric Crozier to collaborate. Meeting the two men at Aldeburgh, reading the story for the first time, and noting their eagerness for a favourable verdict, Crozier pointed out to them its operatic drawbacks: a 1797 shipboard setting hard to stage, a hero with a stammer and, above all, the all-male cast. Crozier also feared, but did not (and probably dared not) say so, 'this inherently homosexual subject'.[5] Though this is never spelled out in Melville's original, or the opera's final libretto, Billy is called 'Beauty' by his shipmates and his charm and looks affect both his evil master-at-arms and his honourable captain, Edward Fairfax Vere. Indeed, when Vere realises that he must hang Billy for a crime of which he is morally innocent (unable to defend himself because of his stammer, he strikes and accidentally kills Claggart for falsely accusing him of mutiny), he declares passionately that he must destroy 'Beauty, handsomeness, goodness'. Indeed, the opera's ultimate message is that Billy's goodness redeems Vere, who sings in the epilogue that 'he has saved me, and blessed me, and the love that passes understanding has come to me'.

Britten began composing *Billy Budd* in February 1950, but while Crozier had come around to feeling that it could be a 'stupendous' opera', the composer now began to have doubts. According to Crozier, in a letter to Nancy Evans, he went through

'a period of revulsion against *Billy Budd*, from a misunderstanding about the purpose of the story, and he wanted to give the whole thing up. But now he has come through and he sees that his feeling was muddled, and with that change everything has improved, health, temper, outlook...'

Billy Budd went into rehearsal at Covent Garden in the autumn of 1951. The title role was sung by the young American baritone Theodor Uppman, a fine singer who also looked the part. The producer was Basil Coleman (henceforth a valued friend and associate), John Piper designed and Britten himself conducted.[6] Peter Pears sang the role of Vere, and said later, 'That was my part, that was me', feeling too that the opera's central figure was Vere, who had 'the main moral problem...he could have saved Billy, and yet circumstances forced him to sacrifice him.' Using Piper's skilful set, in which balsa wood arches suggested the ship's ribs, Coleman managed the production skilfully as well as finding Britten 'remarkable to work with...gradually the cast responded to the words and music and became more and more involved in the moving story.' *Billy Budd* is dedicated to George and Marion Harewood, and the composer told them, 'It is by far the biggest, & I think the best, piece I've written for some time.'

The première of *Billy Budd* took place on 1 December 1951. The composer was pleased with the production, and though he later revised the score, compressing four acts into two, the opera remained dear to him. However, as so often, press reaction was mixed. In *The Times*, Britten's occasional adversary Frank Howes called this the Britten opera he had waited for, sounding 'the deeper music of humanity', while Sir Kenneth Clark described it as 'one of the great masterpieces that change human conduct'. Yet elsewhere it was called 'flawed' and 'purposeless'. As usual, the composer noticed only the adverse criticism, writing to Lennox Berkeley of 'those dreary middlebrows who don't know what to think till they read the *New Statesman!*'. In that journal, Desmond Shawe-Taylor had written that 'the opera as a whole does not quite fulfil the hopes I had built on it'. In the same letter to Berkeley, Britten wrote that he avoided reading the views of critics, since they made him angry: 'What a race – vermin, living off others' leavings!' Peter Pears said later:

'Ben of course did mind, in the sense that to see one's own children spat at in public is a disagreeable experience. But it didn't last too long. He expected it, after a time...[But] the press all along – I mean, who trusts the press? His opinion of critics was very, very low.'

Today, *Billy Budd* is popular and often performed, although expensive to stage. But in 1951 there were understandable reasons for critical reserve. Clearly the all-male cast was a hostage to fortune, and so was the salt-sea orchestration, in which, as Erwin Stein first noted, the first woodwind players have even more to do than the first violins. Ultimately, though, it was less the music than the story and its treatment which upset some people: even among Britten's friends. Joan Cross and Michael Tippett reacted similarly in disliking its element of cruelty. Others were disturbed by the way that Billy's hanging was presented with more than a hint of the Crucifixion, particularly in view of the story's sexual undertones. A few people went so far as to call *Budd* 'The Bugger's Opera': among them, sadly, was John Ireland, himself attracted to boys and thus in no position to throw stones. (When Britten composed a later opera, *The Turn of the Screw*, another name emerged, '*The Stern of the Crew*'.)

A publicity photograph of Britten and Pears taken in Vienna in 1952.

Yet with this opera behind him, Britten's thoughts turned to yet another. Shortly after the death of George VI in March 1952, while he was with the Harewoods on an Austrian skiing holiday, the idea came up of a new work that might mark the dawning of a second Elizabethan age. Back in London, the proposed commission received royal approval and, this time, the composer chose for his librettist the South African born writer William Plomer, ten years older than he, a friend of

Forster and – though very discreetly – also homosexual; this quiet man looking 'like a cross between a doctor and an army chaplain' had lectured at the Aldeburgh Festival and proved congenial. They settled on the story of the first Queen Elizabeth and her favourite, the Earl of Essex, as treated in 1928 by Lytton Strachey. Joan Cross, now in her early fifties, would play the ageing queen, torn between love and duty, and Pears would be Essex, the impulsive courtier whose wayward ambition was to cost him his life. John Piper and Basil Coleman were the other principal collaborators. The opera was to be called *Gloriana* and the date of the première was fixed for 8 June 1953 as part of Queen Elizabeth II's coronation celebrations. With Imogen Holst, who had come to Aldeburgh in 1952 to act as his assistant and dealt with many musical matters short of actual composition, Britten settled down to writing his new opera in the autumn of 1952 and completed his score on 13 March 1953. The work was dedicated to the new Queen, 'by gracious permission'.

As William Plomer has said, *Gloriana* concerned the Queen both in public and in private, so that we saw 'the lonely woman's longing for a close human relationship and her fear of its possible consequences for her people and her country...her sense of her own power and her humility before God'. Though few noticed it at the time, for the two operas are otherwise so different, there is a parallel between her situation in having to sign Essex's death-warrant and that of Vere in *Budd*. *Gloriana* resembles *Budd*, too, in offering both grand spectacle and intimate psychological drama: the spectacle here is of pageantry, ceremony and costume in such scenes as the Norwich masque and the Whitehall Palace dance, while the intimacy lies in the insight the opera gives us into the queen's heart.

The production of *Gloriana* was both lavish and fine, and, accoring to Basil Coleman, Joan Cross gave 'a great performance' in the title role. Yet its coronation gala première was virtually a failure. William Plomer later called its reception 'curiously mixed', but privately used the word 'hostile', remembering that at the final curtain, he and Britten heard 'no more than a cool sprinkling of applause' and that Britten leaned over from their box above the stalls muttering, 'Clap, damn you, clap!'. Part of the trouble was the muted ending, with the dying queen alone on stage, but the chief problem was the stiff audience of unmusical state dignitaries who would have much preferred a jolly pageant: in the foyer, someone was heard referring to the

A scene from *Gloriana*. Joan Cross, centre, sings the role of Elizabeth I. To her right is Peter Pears in the role of the Earl of Essex.

opera as 'by this Benjamin Bradford, about Queen Elizabeth and Lord Darnley'. Quoting bitterly from Voltaire, Plomer commented: 'Alas, the ears of the mighty are often mighty long ears'. Lord Harewood has called this first night 'one of the great disasters of operatic history' – though that is too harsh.

This ignorant audience gave a cue to some critics who should have known better, and the journal *Musical Opinion* crudely joked, 'Sic transit *Gloriana*'. In the *Sunday Times*, Ernest Newman wrote more responsibly, but still declared that 'the music seems to me to fall far below the level we have come to expect from a composer of Mr Britten's gifts.' The composer's reaction was abrupt and typical: 'If I had listened to the critics I would have given up writing about music long ago.' However, this was not the whole story. *The Times* wrote of 'superb richness and invention' and the *Observer* of 'a variety of musical splendours', while the *Manchester Guardian* noted 'the clear demonstration, clearer even than in Britten's previous operas, of the Verdian quality, in the sense both of kind and of power, of his genius.' Finally, Vaughan Williams, now 80 and the respected senior figure in British music, declared in a letter to *The Times* that the sovereign's commission to a British composer should be a matter of national pride, adding, 'Those who cavil at the public expense involved should realise what such a gesture means to the prestige of our own music.' In the *Spectator*, Martin Cooper, regretting the 'almost sadistic relish' with which *Gloriana* had been castigated, commented that 'the fashion has changed and it is now smart to underrate Britten's music...He has been ill-served, with the best of intentions, by a fanatical clique of admirers.' In other words, some commentators still preferred to believe that his success was largely due to knowing the right people, whether in the arts or in society; there were still hints, too, of a homosexual mafia powerful in the British establishment.

Later audiences at Covent Garden liked *Gloriana* better, and so did others when the opera went on tour. But it was 13 years before a new Sadler's Wells production in 1966 enabled it to find its way into the repertory. On that later occasion, Britten had almost to drag William Plomer on to the stage to share in the curtain calls, and Plomer wrote later, 'I was thinking of the long delay in the recognition of *Gloriana*, and kept a grave face.'

Even though its reception had been lukewarm, *Gloriana* marked a milestone in Britten's career. He was created a Companion of Honour on 1 June 1953, so joining an exclusive order limited to 65 members. At 39, he was also exceptionally young to receive this honour. Twelve years later, he was to receive the Order of Merit, limited to 24 members, and in the year of his death he was created a life peer as Baron Britten of Aldeburgh, an honour never before accorded to a composer. Inevitably, from the time of *Gloriana* onwards, there were those who criticised him for, as they saw it, abandoning his youthful radicalism to become an establishment figure. Worse still, they insinuated that he was an opportunistic courtier whose friendship with the Queen's cousin Lord Harewood had more to do with ambition than affection. He knew what was said. Nevertheless, he accepted these honours which enhanced the status of his art and profession, and since he believed that artists should serve the society in which they lived, it was probably right for him to do so. In any case, there was never any chance that he would take them as an excuse to become complacent.

(1) These are indications of pace and show the number of beats to the minute.

(2) However, he and Britten always maintained a London pied-à-terre.

(3) She was the daughter of Erwin Stein (1885-1958), who met Britten in Vienna in 1934 and then worked for Boosey & Hawkes in London, where the composer's music was his special concern. From 1946, he and his

family occupied a flat in Pears's London house, where Britten called them 'almost second Mayers'. In 1949, Marion Stein married the Earl of Harewood, an admirer of Britten's music and President of the Aldeburgh Festival; their marriage was dissolved in 1967 and in 1973 she married the then Liberal Party leader Jeremy Thorpe. In 1985 Mrs Thorpe became a Trustee of the Britten-Pears Foundation.

(4) He told Elizabeth Mayer that 'neither Joan Cross nor Peter should sing any more on the stage' and wrote a letter to the composer, which, according to his fellow poet Stephen Spender, Britten returned torn into pieces.

(5) Forster was himself homosexual, and, according to Humphrey Carpenter, intended *Billy Budd* 'to be a tract on the redeeming power of homosexual love, with Billy as a specimen of lower-class goodness, like Alec Scudder in his then unpublished novel *Maurice* which he showed to Britten and Pears, destroying the "perverted" aspect of homosexuality (Claggart) and becoming a saviour-figure to the rest of the ship'. In a letter to Britten after the opera was completed, he called it 'my Nunc Dimittis'.

(6) Though only as a last-minute substitution for Josef Krips, who found himself unable to use the photocopied score.

Chapter 7

West meets East

Receiving the Freedom of the Borough of Lowestoft in 1951, Britten said:

'As an artist, I want to serve the community. In other days, artists were the servants of institutions like the Church, or of private patrons. Today it is the community that orders the artist about. It is not a bad thing to try to serve all sorts of different people and to have to work to order. Any artist worth his salt has...ideas knocking about in his head, and an invitation to write something can often direct these ideas into a concrete form and shape. Of course, it can sometimes be difficult when one doesn't feel in the mood, but perhaps that's good for one, too! – anyhow, composers (like other people) can be horribly lazy, and often this is the only way that they can be made to produce something!'

Interviewed for a television documentary 16 years later, the composer described his methods and a schedule essentially unchanged since he worked on *Peter Grimes:*

'The feeling is that the creator, the artist, has a moment of sudden inspiration, and dashes to the paper or canvas and, in the height of inspiration, writes down or paints this wonderful picture that is in his mind. In my experience, that isn't the way I work. I like working to an exact timetable. I often thank my stars that I had a rather conventional upbringing, that I went to a rather strict school where one was made to work. And I can without much difficulty sit down at nine o'clock in the morning and work straight through the morning until lunchtime. I don't say I always enjoy the work at that time, but it isn't a great struggle to do so each day. I find, actually, that the day divides up quite naturally into three or four periods: the morning, when as I've said, I work till lunchtime, then in the afternoon letters – or, rather more important, is that I go for a walk, where I plan out what I'm going to write in the next period at my desk. I then come back. After tea, up to my studio and work through until about eight o'clock. After dinner I usually find I'm too sleepy to do much more than to read a little bit, and then go to bed rather early.

The mention of reading in this last sentence reminds us that Britten retained his interest in the other arts while allowing himself little leisure to enjoy them. He read both old and new poetry, and his keen literary taste is reflected in his choice of texts for his song cycles as well as operatic scenarios. Among novelists, he liked Forster and Dickens ('I try to read at least one of his novels a year'), and although seldom at the theatre, read some contemporary plays and was 'struck by the similarities they have with libretti'. Though he once proudly showed me a small Constable canvas given him by an admirer, he did not share Peter Pears's passionate interest in painting, and the many

A painting of Aldeburgh Parish Church, owned by the composer. It was painted by his friend John Piper.

original pictures gracing his Aldeburgh home were mostly the singer's: they included canvases by Sickert, Lear, Lamb and Piper as well as their friend Mary Potter. As for architecture, Britten took a lifelong interest in small churches, whether in Suffolk or in Venice – where he and Pears claimed to know most of them. Though his hobbies were few, he was a keen and knowledgeable birdwatcher, and one of the few things that he allowed to interrupt his work at Aldeburgh was the sight of a rare bird which he would study with binoculars. He also enjoyed driving classic cars (over the years, he owned Rolls-Royces, a Jensen and an Alvis), and considered this his only personal extravagance. His sports included tennis and table tennis – and he liked to win.

The regular meals punctuating Britten's schedule are, of course, familiar landmarks in a working day and often taken for granted. Yet they are difficult for a person who works at home and has no one responsible for the quiet, necessary household routines of shopping and cooking, cleaning and washing clothes. Britten was never one to work, like John Ireland (or even Beethoven), in bachelor squalor, eating out or irregularly, surrounded by dirty crockery and leaving an unmade bed. On the other hand, he had little aptitude for household tasks, as Peter Pears recalled:

'Ben was not a well-trained domestic animal, I think. He could boil an egg...but that was about as far as he'd go. He could have watched a piece of toast, I suppose, being burnt slowly. If he made his bed he made a mess of it; I mean, he did frequently make his bed, but it wasn't very comfortably made and somebody would probably have to come along and make it again for him afterwards. He liked a family life...a regular household life, to run on fairly sure rails. Ben was never a Bohemian, in any sense of the word. He really was a working musician – a working composer.'

For some 20 years, the person who did Britten's household chores was his housekeeper Nellie Hudson, who retired in 1973 to a cottage that he and Pears built for her. The niece of a Snape miller, she entered their service knowing that they were more than 'just concert people' and therefore respectable. In a 1979 interview, she said that she had regarded her job as 'mothering Mr Britten', but kept at a proper distance from her employer. He liked her home cooking – nursery food, Pears called it – and his favourite dishes included a 'nice, creamy milk pudding', 'spotted dog' and dark treacle jelly. 'But Mr Britten had to be careful', she said, 'because he hadn't got a strong inside like Mr Pears had': the singer liked spicy food and sometimes brought home recipes from foreign tours. Miss Hudson could produce appetising food at all hours, sometimes catering for Aldeburgh Festival committee meetings, which in early days, according to Imogen Holst, 'often went on until midnight [and] had a way of turning into parties, with home-bottled wine fetched from the cellar and poured out by candle-light'. She would also see her employer off on a concert tour, asking him, 'Have you got your passport, your money, all the music?' – and then welcome him back to a warm home.

After *Gloriana*, Britten's next composition was a song cycle to eight Thomas Hardy poems, 'Winter Words', and Peter Pears and he performed it for the first time at Harewood House in

Nellie Hudson, Britten's housekeeper, at Cosy Nook, in the gardens of The Red House.

Britten and Pears in Venice during rehearsals for *The Turn of the Screw* in 1954. John and Myfanwy Piper are in the foreground with their children Clarissa and Edward behind. Basil Douglas sits at right.

October 1953. The cycle has a rich humanity and a keen response to natural beauty, although ending with the serious, deeply questioning song *'Before Life and After'*. He dedicated it to John Piper and his wife Myfanwy. The Pipers were both to be closely involved with his next opera, commissioned by the 1954 Biennale Festival in Venice. Since it was to be another chamber opera for the English Opera Group (having the same relationship to grand opera, he said, as a string quartet to a symphony), the subject had to be intimate, and Britten decided on Henry James's ghost story, 'The Turn of the Screw', which he had known since hearing it as a radio play in 1932 and finding it 'wonderful' but 'terribly eerie and scarey'. Myfanwy Piper now suggested it and Britten, agreeing, asked her to write the libretto: an unexpected choice, since, although a sensitive and cultured woman who had read English at Oxford, she was not a professional writer. But as usual, the composer's instinct was right and she did an excellent job.[1] She, in her turn, found him 'very easy to work with, because he knew what he wanted.'

Britten should have begun work on *The Turn of the Screw* in the autumn of 1953, but instead fell ill with bursitis, an inflammation of the bursal sac in his right shoulder. He had to cancel all playing and conducting, and drove a left-hand-drive Mercedes, but still managed to do some composition, telling his friends the Mauds, 'I'm getting on well with my left-handed music writing'. What caused his condition is unknown: it may have been the muscular tension that he suffered when conducting, but Humphrey Carpenter feels that he may also have been frightened of beginning work on the opera. James's story of Miles and Flora, two children in a remote country house who may have been sexually corrupted by Peter Quint, a manservant, now dead, was bound to cause further murmurs among Britten's detractors. [2]

None the less, Britten was greatly drawn to James's novella. Set in a 19th-century country house called Bly, it portrays a young and inexperienced governess who, having been placed in sole charge, realises that some evil has occurred there and resolves to save her beloved charges, Miles and Flora, from the ghosts of a former valet, Peter Quint, and her own unhappy predecessor, Miss Jessel, whom she believes to be seeking possession of the children's souls. There has been controversy as to whether James intended his readers to believe in the ghosts or let them wonder if they exist only in the mind of the overwrought governess. Britten, however, insisted that they should be real in his opera, visible to the audience and singing words which his librettist had to invent, giving them a scene to themselves at the start of Act 2. He began composing *The Turn of the Screw* at the end of March 1954, five months before the première, but once he was under way, progressed quickly. One section, the brisk 13-part fugue of Act 1, Variation 5, was composed on a train between Ipswich and London. The Venice fee was big enough to allow a month of rehearsals in Suffolk, and a strong cast was assembled, with Jennifer Vyvyan as the Governess, Joan Cross as the elderly housekeeper Mrs Grose, and Peter Pears and the Greek-Armenian soprano Arda Mandikian (who possessed a dark, distinctive vocal timbre) as the ghosts.

A scene from *The Turn of the Screw*, with Olive Dyer, left, as Flora, Jennifer Vyvyan as the Governess and David Hemmings as Miles.

Casting the children created a problem, but a slightly-built adult singer, Olive Dyer, was found to play Flora. As for Miles, the choice fell on the 12-year-old David Hemmings, who possessed 'a true but very small treble voice', writes Basil Coleman, who produced.

David Hemmings had looks, personality and acting talent (he went on to a film career), and soon attracted Britten's attention. The English Opera Group's manager, Basil Douglas, was later to say that the composer was 'really smitten...and didn't David know it!', and indeed 'in love with him, but as far as I know there was nothing more. Ben was very self-restrained.' At one point Peter Pears became alarmed, but managed to calm matters down, behaving, according to observers, with sympathy and understanding.

David Hemmings, who stayed in Britten's house, has since said that he recognised Britten's affection but knew that he was 'a gentleman' and 'a deeply considerate father figure...in all of the time that I spent with him he never abused that trust' – although 'the intensity of Aldeburgh somehow became entanged with Bly':

'Did he kiss me? Yes, he did. But that was more my need as a young boy alone in his house than it was any threat. I slept in his bed, when I was frightened, and I still felt no sexual threat whatsoever. And I think it would have embarrassed him a damn sight more than it would have embarrassed me at the time...Of all the people I have worked with, I count my relationship with Ben to have been one of the finest. And also my relationship with Peter too...there is no man in my entire life that has been more influential on my attitudes than Ben.'

Britten was more than usually nervous at the première of *The Turn of the Screw*, on 14 September 1954. But it was a success, in the small Teatro la Fenice with roses placed in each box and filling it with a scent suiting the country-house setting. As for critical reaction, Frank Howes in *The Times* wondered as to the subject-matter but noted that the composer's musical ability was 'equal to any demands made on it'. In the *Sunday Times*, Felix Aprahamian thought this opera to be his finest achievement yet. However, Antoine Golea in the Paris paper *L'Express* called it a parable of 'homosexual love and the futility of struggling against it' – almost certainly the first time that homosexuality was mentioned in print in the context of Britten's work.

After these performances in Venice, Britten, Pears, Basil Coleman and Imogen Holst travelled back to England in the composer's Rolls and *The Turn of the Screw* was staged at Sadler's Wells before touring to Holland and Sweden. Decca recorded it in January 1955, and it became the first Britten opera to be recorded complete, in the still newish format of the long-playing record and on two 12-inch vinyl discs. In the meantime, John Ireland had saluted it in a letter to a friend as

'the most remarkable and original music I have ever heard from a British composer...what he has accomplished in sound by the use of only 13 instruments was, to me, inexplicable, almost miraculous. This is not to say I liked the music, but it is gripping, vital and often terrifying. I am now (perhaps reluctantly) compelled to regard Britten as possessing ten times the musical talent, intuition and ability of all other living British composers put together.'

In November 1954, Britten and Pears drove down to North Lancing, in Sussex, to spend a quiet weekend with Pears's old friend Esther Neville-Smith, the widow of a former master at his school, Lancing College, and the commissioner of *Saint Nicolas* (for which she paid just £100). Partly as a result of a recommendation from Britten, of which I then knew nothing, I was in my first term teaching music at Lancing and lodged at her charming old house, Friar's Acre. I remember a delicious dinner that she produced from her tiny kitchen for the three of us and the relaxed fireside conversation afterwards. William Plomer came over one evening from his home nearby, and when Britten drove him back in Peter Pears's Morris Traveller, I went along for the ride. Returning home and garaging the car, he said he thought *The Turn of the Screw* his best piece so far, along with his most recent canticle, 'Still Falls the Rain', to an Edith Sitwell text, which was then awaiting its first performance. (Later, he told Sitwell that these two works made him feel 'on the threshold of a new musical world.') However, he added that writing the opera had been difficult, 'like finding things for people to do in a house party, or squeezing toothpaste out of a tube that's nearly finished' – remarks presumably referring to its unique variation form and its economy of musical means. That Christmas, Esther stayed with Britten and Pears at Aldeburgh and wrote from there to tell me that it had been 'Such a lovely time!'. Sadly, three months later she died in a road accident, and they drove down to Sussex in Britten's Rolls-Royce to attend her funeral.

It was always difficult, Pears would say, to get Britten to go on holiday. Yet they did enjoy many holidays together, often with other friends. There were visits to Italy, where Britten liked the sunshine and Mediterranean light: Venice – even when cold and out of season – was always a favourite place, and another journey took them by flying boat to Sicily. One summer, with the Aldeburgh fisherman Billy Burrell, they made up a party that sailed in a 13-ton launch across the North Sea and along the Rhine. There were a few skiing holidays and gentle motoring tours through France. The composer seems to have appreciated these periods of relaxation, although he rarely left his work wholly behind and his creative processes went on in his head. Sometimes, also, relaxation could be fitted into or added to an operatic or concert tour.

In October 1955, Britten and Pears commenced a months-long tour which was also to incorporate a memorable and artistically fruitful holiday. After a busy opera season and a series of recordings that included *The Turn of the Screw, Saint Nicolas, The Little Sweep,* and a recital of English songs with Pears, they set off on a lengthy concert tour-cum-holiday that took them further than ever before. They performed first in Europe, moving steadily eastwards and seeing *Peter Grimes* in the Croatian capital of Zagreb before spending nine days in Turkey. Then, on 11 December, they flew to Karachi, after which there were further engagements in Bombay, Delhi – they spent Christmas at Agra and saw the Taj Mahal by moonlight – and Calcutta. Next came Singapore, which Pears considered 'a very "homey" corner of the Empire!'. There they were joined by the Prince and Princess of Hesse, friends whom they had met not long before through the Harewoods and were already close and valued. Margaret ('Peg') Hesse was Scottish-born; she and her husband Ludwig ('Lu') had married in Britain before the war at a ceremony overshadowed by an air accident in which several of his family were killed. A wealthy, cultured couple, without children to keep them at home, they were ready to join the musicians in visiting a part of the world which none of them knew well. Furthermore, the Prince was a poet who, according to his wife, found an immediate rapport with the composer.

The composer on holiday in Bali in 1956.

Now came the most exciting period of the tour. The recitals that Pears and Britten gave in the main cities of Indonesia led at last to a real holiday in Bali. They reached that magic island on 12 January 1956 and seem to have agreed with the Indian statesman Pandit Nehru's description of it as 'like the morning of the world'.

Britten had already come across Balinese music in America, and here, in its proper setting, it thrilled him. He told his godson Roger Duncan, the son of Ronald Duncan and then aged 13:

'The sun is already up, and it is as warm as a lovely English mid-day...Even at this hour there is the sound of a musical gong; in fact the air is always filled with the sound of native music – flutes, xylophones, metalphones [3] and extraordinary booming gongs – just as it is filled by the oddest spicey smells, of flowers, of trees, and of cooking, as one's eye is filled by similar sights plus that of the really most beautiful people, of a lovely dark brown colour, sweet pathetic expressive faces, wearing strange clothes, sarongs of vivid colours, and sometimes wearing nothing at all. Sorry, old boy, to write in this 'high-falutin' way, but one is really knocked sideways...'

A photograph taken by Peter Pears of a Balinese child being taught to dance. A gamelan orchestra is seen in the background.

As the party was taken by a resident Dutch scholar to gamelan orchestra performances, shadow puppet plays, cremations (colourful, noisy ceremonies) and the like, Britten began to grasp some of the principles of Balinese music, and told Imogen Holst that he found it 'fantastically rich – melodically, rhythmically, texture (such orchestration!!) & above all formally. It is a remarkable culture [and] a bewildering richness. At last I'm beginning to catch on to the technique, but it's about as complicated as Schönberg.'

In this place, as near to an earthly Paradise as they could imagine, Britten, Pears and the Hesses swam, lazed and drank palm wine, and also dressed up in local costume for a photo in which, according to Peg Hesse, Britten 'looked like a governess at a fancy dress' and Pears resembled one of Wagner's Rhinemaidens. Though a typical Balinese lavatory reminded Britten of 'a late work of his friend Henry Moore', nobody minded. They left Bali on 25 January to resume the concert tour, reaching Hong Kong on 2 February and Tokyo six days later. There Britten conducted performances of the *Sinfonia da Requiem, Les illuminations* and *The Young Person's Guide to the Orchestra*. However, his most exciting and fruitful musical experience was that of seeing the classical Noh drama, *Sumidagawa*, which portrays a woman mourning for her lost child. The action was slow and the vocal style of the all-male cast strange, but when Britten's host asked the composer if he wished to slip away, 'Ben started as if from a trance, and said, "What? Leave this? I couldn't possibly."' After this, the composer acquired a recording of Sumidagawa and transcriptions of Japanese music. Later, he told William Plomer, who knew Japan and had suggested his seeing a Noh play, of his 'incredibly strong reactions'; and in 1964 the two of them were to use *Sumidagawa* as the basis for the church parable *Curlew River*, a work reflecting Britten's response to what he called this 'totally new "operatic" experience'.

As for Balinese music, this was to influence him in several works. The first of these occupied him in 1956 and was a full-length ballet for Covent Garden called *The Prince of the Pagodas*. He had thought about it before leaving on his tour, and its oriental subject had stimulated him to make notes; even so, he found the task of writing this 125-minute orchestral score far more arduous than he had expected, remarking, 'I've never written so many notes in my life – all those bits of thistledown dancing on the stage actually need a tremendous amount of music.' Eventually he secured a postponement of the première scheduled for September, and it finally took place on New Year's Day, 1957. The choreographer was John Cranko, the designer John Piper, and the principal dancers Svetlana Beriosova and David Blair. Britten conducted and was presented with a giant laurel wreath.

In writing this ballet, his longest purely instrumental work, Britten took Tchaikovsky as his model, but although this was surely to the good, its quality remains controversial. For Donald Mitchell, 'Britten's genius burns at its very brightest...it might be said that the *Pagodas* combines the loose build and, on occasion, festal atmosphere of *Gloriana* with the concentrated, total thematic organisation of *The Turn of the Screw*; yet Michael Kennedy calls it 'a utilitarian score...of all Britten's large-scale works it seems to me to be the least characteristic'. Maybe it sometimes betrays the speed at which it was written, for as Mitchell suggests, the composer 'had his back to the wall' towards the end of his huge task and working with the ballet world left him 'bruised and debilitated'. This weariness doubtless contributed to his subsequent edgy attitude to his music, which he later referred to, in a letter to Erwin Stein, as 'that beastly work'. But much of it is thrilling and the sound has a rare brilliance, not least (but also not only) in the tinkling gamelan imitations in Princess Belle Rose's Pagoda Land scene in which animated miniature pagodas revolve. Britten recorded a slightly abridged version of *The Prince of the Pagodas* just after the première, but it had to wait until 1989 for a complete recording.

Britten produced no further composition until towards the end of 1957, when he wrote his *Songs from the Chinese* for Peter Pears and the guitarist Julian Bream – an epigrammatic, elegant cycle that is arguably also a by-product of his visit to the Far East, although he never saw China itself. Instead he took a spring holiday in Italy with Pears and the Hesses, and, in June, saw *Albert Herring* celebrate his tenth anniversary at the tenth Aldeburgh Festival. In August, he took the English Opera Group and *The Turn of the Screw* to Stratford, Ontario, and then he and Pears travelled to Berlin for a recital and more performances of the opera. But this was also a financially worrying time for the Group, as he told Basil Coleman ('we've performed less and less and the administrative costs soar'), and he decided to dismiss some hitherto valued colleagues, charging its manager, Basil Douglas, with the task of breaking the news to them. Douglas now recalls that he 'became awfully unpopular...I never met a more ruthless person than Ben'. Within a few months, Douglas himself was dropped, and this time it was Imogen Holst who had to break the bad news.

The composer with his friend, Mary Potter, the painter. Both are in costume for an English Opera Group ball at the Royal Festival Hall, London, in 1952.

Also in Aldeburgh, Britten moved to a new house in November, exchanging houses (with little money changing hands) with his painter friend Mary Potter; separated from her husband and with children now grown up, she had found her converted farmhouse overlooking Aldeburgh's golf course too big for her and one of her sons suggested the move. Britten, too, was glad to find a home that was still in his beloved Aldeburgh but more secluded from an increasingly curious public. The Red House was large, with a tennis court and vegetable garden, and while he lost his sea view he could still swim in the small pool that he soon built; it was surrounded by a wall so that he could do so nude.[4]

Before moving house, Britten had already begun work on a new short opera for the next Aldeburgh Festival. Eric Crozier had suggested the Chester Miracle Play, *Noye's Fludde*, a 16th-century text giving a colourful account of the Biblical tale with a sprinkling of humour in the persons of the formidable Mrs Noye and her gossipy drinking companions. The composer completed this score a week before Christmas, and the première was given in Orford Church on 18 June 1958. Charles Mackerras conducted and the young producer was Colin

From a production of *Noye's Fludde*, with Owen Brannigan in the role of Noye.

Orford Church, where *Noye's Fludde* received its premiere in June 1958.

Graham. The choice of a church location was deliberate in view of the opera's religious origins. Also following some precedent, most of the performers were children, although the roles of Noye and his wife are professional. These children are both 'on stage' and in the orchestra, which was visible to the side of the action and included recorders, strings, handbells, bugles and percussion. Drawing on local skills, Britten wrote the handbell parts for children of Leiston Modern School and the bugles' music for a school group at Holbrook. He invented a special instrument for the percussionists from Woolverstone Hall, mugs strung in a row which, when struck with a wooden spoon, gave vaguely different notes intended to suggest raindrops on the roof of the Ark. Schoolchildren also played the many animals taken into the Ark – 'camelles', 'doggës', 'cattës', squeaking mice and so on. The audience also 'performs' by participating in three hymns. Thus, *Noye's Fludde* was not created for a sophisticated visiting audience but to foster local participation and involvement. Even so, it has proved to have a striking universality. Lord Clark wrote of this simple yet profound piece:

'To sit in Orford Church, where I had spent so many hours of my childhood dutifully awaiting some spark of divine fire, and then to receive it at last in the performance of *Noye's Fludde*, was an overwhelming experience.'

That year, Britten and Imogen Holst collaborated on a children's book called 'The Story of Music' (the title was later changed to 'The Wonderful World of Music'). She did most of the writing, but the book certainly reflects Britten's thought. For example, on the matter of 'nature versus art', he wrote to suggest the phrase, 'an artist...has to create something that will have a life of its own, with the vitality of Nature's own creations'. On the post-Webernian serialism that was now gaining ground, the authors offered a cautious objectivity: 'Some think that it does not matter what style a composer chooses to write in, as long as he has something definite to say and says it clearly'. Despite this, Britten cared little for rigorously applied serialism and soon afterwards spoke out more frankly:

'I am seriously disturbed by its limitations. I can see it taking no part in the music-lover's music-making. Its methods make writing gratefully for voices or instruments an impossibility, which inhibits amateurs and children. I find it worrying that our contemporary young composers are not able to write things for the young or amateurs to play and sing.'

Yet Britten never closed his mind to serialism, as the twelve-note fundamental theme in *The Turn of the Screw* shows, and was always prepared to draw upon its methods in a personal way. Thus we also find serial procedures in his operas *A Midsummer Night's Dream* (where a motto theme of four chords uses all twelve pitches of the chromatic scale), *Owen Wingrave* and *Death in Venice*. In an interview published in 1963, he was to say:

'For example, my Nocturne opens with a long vocal melisma descending, and it closes with its inversion ascending, but I would consider it no great virtue consciously to know that. All that is important is that the composer should make his music sound inevitable and right; the system is unimportant.'

The work Britten refers to here is his *Nocturne* for tenor and chamber orchestra. A companion piece to the *Serenade* with its poetic theme of evening, its texts (by eight poets) deal instead with night and dreams. However, here too the cycle ends with a sonnet, Shakespeare's profound love poem 'When most I wink'. It is more sombre than the Serenade: as Britten later said in a broadcast interview, the night 'can release many things which one thinks had better not be released', and he called his setting of Wordsworth here, which describes a dream about the French Revolution, 'very nightmarish'. To Marion Harewood, he wrote of this new cycle, 'it is the strangest & remotest thing – but then dreams are strange and remote'. Nevertheless, much of it is lyrical and sensuously beautiful. Peter Pears gave its première on 16 October 1958, in Leeds Town Hall. Five weeks later, he and Britten performed another new cycle, this time for voice and piano. Shorter than the Nocturne, it consists of settings of poems by Hölderlin and was a 50th birthday present for Lu Hesse: the première was at the Hesses' palatial 'hunting lodge' near Frankfurt, Schloss Wolfsgarten. The composer was soon to say of these songs: 'They are short – just fragments...but I believe they are probably my best vocal works so far.'

In 1959, Britten received an honorary doctorate in music from Cambridge, one of many such university honours which came his way. Appropriately, he also now wrote a *Cantata academica* commissioned by Basle University. One of his most exuberant and celebratory works, it belies its solemn-sounding name despite his use of the ingenious musical devices of inversion, canon, fugue, and even (in one warmly flowing theme) serialism. Although he admitted to being not especially interested in this 'chore' of a commission, the music does not show it. Soon after this was finished, he visited William Plomer and they talked further about their proposed Noh-based opera, now provisionally called *The River*, though he did not yet begin its composition. Instead he provided a strikingly intense *Missa Brevis* for boys' choir and organ for the trebles of Westminster Cathedral and their choirmaster George Malcolm.

At Aldeburgh, Britten and his Festival associates decided to enlarge and improve the Jubilee Hall during that winter, at a cost of £18,000, and the composer agreed to write a new opera to be given there in 1960. Some months later, he wrote:

'As this was a comparatively sudden decision there was no time to get a libretto written, so we took one that was ready to hand...I have always loved *A Midsummer Night's Dream*.'

Peter Pears, John Cranko and Benjamin Britten in front of the Jubilee Hall during rebuilding for the premiere of *A Midsummer Night's Dream*.

The Jubilee Hall before enlargement and improvement.

There was time for a brief holiday in Venice before starting work, with Peter Pears, on the adaptation (and necessary curtailment, mainly of the early scenes) of Shakespeare's play. Britten then set to work on his score, starting in October and finishing in April 1960 – 'the fastest of any big opera I have written'. This was despite gastric 'flu and some recurrence of his old arm trouble. In February he wrote to Pears, 'The cold's got into the sinuses, & I stream from nose & eyes, & can't breathe or hear...However I'm pushing on with the score.' Later he wrote, 'I find that one's inclination, whether one wants to work or not, does not in the least affect the quality.'

Produced by John Cranko and with Britten conducting, *A Midsummer Night's Dream* had its première on 11 June 1960 and was an unqualified success.[5] Indeed, the sustained skill of the music, with its three sound-worlds for fairies, lovers and rustics, was at once recognised. Britten's old adversary Frank Howes of *The Times* had no reservations, calling it 'tout court a great English opera'. Of course, this classic comedy had a scenario to which no one could object, and some people were relieved to find 'proper' love duets. However, the musical focus was less on human love than on the mysterious fairy world of Oberon (a counter-tenor role), Puck and Tytania as well as the 'rude mechanicals' led by Bottom. Pears, for whom there was no obvious leading role, played Flute, and thus also Thisbe in the rustics' 'play within a play' – sending up the hammier kind of Italian opera in a way which nearly stole the show. Within a year of the first performance, *The Dream* was given in ten

The composer conducts a rehearsal for *A Midsummer Night's Dream*.

opera houses outside Britain, including that of Tokyo. In 1961, it came to Covent Garden, where Sir John Gielgud produced and Georg Solti conducted.

During 1960, Britten also revised and shortened *Billy Budd*. The BBC broadcast the new two-act version in November and Covent Garden staged it four years later – when Desmond Shawe-Taylor, hitherto a doubter, was amazed that he had not at first recognised this 'self-evident and cast-iron masterpiece'.

Although Britten's music was now widely performed, and he was a familiar performer in the world's opera houses and concert halls, the political 'iron curtain' that separated the European east and west meant that he was less known in the then Soviet Union and his satellites. Even so, he did perform in some of those countries, saying in 1961 that he was 'conscious simply of human beings – how plucky and spirited those people are in Poland and Yugoslavia'. For him, the task of politicians was 'to organise the world and resolve its tensions', and he added, 'I disbelieve profoundly in power and violence'. Despite the prejudices and pressures of the period, in the 1960s he developed an agreeable and fruitful Russian connection, meeting his fellow composer Dmitri Shostakovich and the cellist Mstislav Rostropovich while they visited London for a performance of Shostakovich's First Cello Concerto. Asked to write a sonata by the cellist, Britten agreed and sent him the new work early in 1961. Soon after that, he was again in London and they arranged a run-through. Both were nervous, and, according to Rostropovich, drank 'four or five very large whiskies'

The composer with Mstislav Rostropovich on his right and Dmitri Shostakovich on his left in Moscow in 1963.

103

Wilfrid Owen, the war poet.

before playing, although Peter Pears thought this probably an exaggeration. 'We played like pigs, but we were so happy.' They gave its première at the Aldeburgh Festival on 7 July 1961.

In 1961, Britten composed a major sacred work, his *War Requiem*, for the rebuilt Coventry Cathedral which stands beside the ruins of the medieval one destroyed by wartime bombing. Here, the bitter anti-war poems of Wilfred Owen are placed, by a stroke of imaginative genius, alongside the timeless and universal Latin text of the *Mass for the Dead*. Britten's idea was to make a statement about war's futility and, at the same time, express his sympathy with man's self-inflicted suffering. He preceded his score with Owen's words, 'My subject is War, and the pity of War...all a poet can do is to warn.' As soloists, he chose singers from different countries involved in the Second World War: Pears from Britain, Galina Vishnevskaya (Rostropovich's wife) from the Soviet Union and Dietrich Fischer-Dieskau from Germany. However, this

Britten with the Russian soprano Galina Vishnevskaya.

particular symbol of healed international wounds was not immediately realised, as the Soviet authorities did not permit Vishnevskaya to sing in the Coventry performances on 28 and 30 May 1962; on those occasions, the soprano was Heather Harper although Vishnevskaya sang in the recording, made the following January. Once again, this latest Britten work was hailed as a masterpiece. William Mann, of *The Times*, called it 'the most masterly and nobly imagined work that Britten has ever

A rehearsal for the *War Requiem* in Coventry Cathedral in 1962. Peter Pears stands far right. Seated to his right is Dietrich Fischer-Dieskau. In the foreground, Meredith Davies stands in the podium and the composer is to his right.

given us'. By the end of 1964, it had been performed in more than a dozen foreign cities. Surprisingly, these included Leningrad (today again known by its old name of St Petersburg), where its religious and pacifist content might have seemed unacceptable. Among its Russian admirers was Shostakovich, who, according to Rostropovich, thought it the supreme masterpiece of 20th-century music. It was only Stravinsky who was to comment waspishly on the 'Battle-of-Britten sentiment' which required the listener to have his 'Kleenex at the ready...nothing fails like success' – but this reaction from an elderly master whose own later music was neglected may betray an element of pique. The recording was to sell nearly a quarter of a million copies.

[1] At this time, the critic Desmond Shawe-Taylor compared Britten's changes of librettist to Henry VIII's changes of wife, suggesting, 'it is time to settle down. Can we look for a Catherine Parr...?' In turn, Montagu Slater, Ronald Duncan and Eric Crozier had all felt some hurt at being – as it seemed – discarded by him.

(2) Henry James himself had inclined towards homosexuality and it was now in the public's mind, for in October 1953, the British newspapers mentioned a drive against 'male vice', soon followed by the conviction and imprisonment of Lord Montagu of Beaulieu and two other upper-class men on charges arising from their association with young men. On 15 January, the editor of the *London Evening Standard* told his proprietor, Lord Beaverbrook: 'Scotland Yard are definitely stepping up their activities against the homosexuals. Some weeks ago they interviewed Benjamin Britten. This week I am told they have interviewed Cecil Beaton. No action is to be taken against either.'

(3) The proper term is 'metallophones' and refers to a family of instruments including the celesta and glockenspiel of western orchestras. The Balinese gender belongs to this group; its tuned bronze bars are suspended in a wooden frame and struck with mallets.

(4) His brother Robert, on a visit, asked, 'do you think you really deserve all this?'

(5) The lone dissenting voice, sadly, was that of Auden, whose comment was, 'dreadful! Pure Kensington!'.

Chapter 8

With Aschenbach in Venice

In 1963, Britten was 50. Before his birthday in November, he completed two major works that are very different, the tough and enigmatic *Cello Symphony* for Rostropovich and the vocal *Cantata Misericordium* for the International Red Cross: the latter, on the Good Samaritan parable, has a Latin text speaking to a divided world of understanding and compassion.

The composer on Aldeburgh beach in 1964.

He now visited the Soviet Union for a festival of British music in which his work figured prominently; audiences there heard his *Sinfonia da Requiem*, the orchestral Interludes and Passacaglia from *Peter Grimes* and the *Cello Sonata*, while Peter Pears sang the *Serenade*, *Winter Words* and *Six Hölderlin Fragments*. In a *Pravda* interview he was reported as thinking the Soviet people 'wonderful', and though a contrary opinion would hardly have been printed, Britten and Pears did like their hosts and the feeling was mutual, both personally and artistically. *Peter Grimes* had its first Soviet performance in the following year and in 1965 the Bolshoi theatre put on *A Midsummer Night's Dream*.

In the meantime, this birthday year was marked by various celebratory events. The composer's friend Anthony Gishford edited a *Tribute to Benjamin Britten* in which the French composer Poulenc called Britten 'glorieux comme un jeune Verdi' and Rostropovich wrote that in time people would celebrate his 150th and 200th birthdays – 'I foresee these jubilees and congratulate you in advance.' Oxford University gave him an honorary degree and, on 12 September, an entire Promenade Concert was devoted to his music. A new Sadler's Wells production of *Peter Grimes* was mounted in the following month. On the birthday itself, 22 November, the composer attended a concert performance of *Gloriana* at London's Royal Festival Hall; but tragically, on that same evening President Kennedy was killed and the news darkened the occasion.

Britten took all these tributes with equanimity. It was certainly pleasanter to be praised than the opposite, and Hans Keller was now calling him 'the greatest composer alive'. Yet he was not amenable to being assessed and placed in an aesthetic pigeon-hole by 'critics who are already trying to document today for tomorrow'. He told William Plomer, 'I feel that...these nice things being written are really obituaries', and replied to a warm letter from William Walton, 'I don't think any composer has ever felt less confident than I – especially somehow when the public praise seems to have got rather out of hand!'.

In January 1964, Britten set off with Pears for a rented apartment in the Palazzo Mocenigo in Venice to write *Curlew River*, his Noh-inspired 'parable for church performance'. Indeed, attending Mass in the church of San Giorgio Maggiore and seeing the priests' robing ceremony gave him the idea of the monks' robing that was to be used at the start of his own piece. His producer and designer Colin Graham worked in Venice with him, proposing sequences of stage action on which Britten then based his free-sounding, almost improvisatory music for a small cast of singers and a tiny instrumental ensemble, and on 15 February he told William Plomer:

'It was a slow start, but after that it rushed ahead, & after a little more than a month I am well towards the end. Apart from the usual bits that need clarifying, I am *very* pleased with it.'

In *Curlew River*, the Japanese tale of a distracted noblewoman, seeking her lost child and crossing a river to find his shrine and hear his spirit voice, is transferred to the fenland of medieval England. Britten's score shows how much he had learned from Noh practice: the writing for flute, small drums, bells and gong is evocative indeed, while the daring use of an all-male cast (Pears was to sing the Madwoman) was equally stylised and authentic. There is no conductor: instead the individual performers 'lead' in turn. For the première in Orford Church during the 1964 Aldeburgh Festival, Colin Graham aimed at 'control, clarity, and concentration', and the performance of this intense piece in these surroundings made a profound impression.

Benjamin Britten rehearsing with Mstislav Rostropovich rehearsing at the Moscow Conservatoire in 1964.

Before that, however, Britten had again visited the Soviet Union to conduct the first performance of his *Cello Symphony* on 12 March, with its dedicatee Rostropovich as the soloist, in the Great Hall of the Moscow Conservatory; such was the enthusiasm of students in the gallery that the finale was encored. In Leningrad, he was delighted when students performed parts of the *War Requiem* for him, and surprised how well they knew his music as a whole. He found an equal enthusiasm when he and Pears went to perform in Prague and Budapest a few weeks later. In Budapest, he enjoyed meeting two 12-year-old twins, Zoltán and Gábor Jeney, who between them played flute, violin and piano, and agreed after some persuasion to compose for them his *Gemini Variations* on a theme

Britten with the Jeney twins, Zoltan and Gabor in 1965.

by the Hungarian composer Kodály. These 'most engaging little chaps' were to play the new piece at the 1965 Aldeburgh Festival, with the octogenarian Kodály present as the guest of honour.

At this time Britten changed his publisher. His relations with Boosey & Hawkes had deteriorated since Erwin Stein's death and Decca, now recording much of his music, had also had difficulties with the firm. Early in 1964, Donald Mitchell, working part-time for Boosey's on Britten's recommendation, had been dropped, and the composer began to wonder whether Faber & Faber (for whom Mitchell acted as an adviser on music books) might go into music publishing. When the firm's chairman agreed, Britten moved to them at once, and they published *Curlew River* and a *Nocturnal* for guitar composed for Julian Bream in 1963 (a sombre meditation on Dowland's song 'Come, heavy sleep'). Another change came in June 1964, when Imogen Holst retired from being his assistant and her former pupil Rosamund Strode took over; she was to remain with him until his death 12 years later.

In July 1964, Britten went to Aspen, Colorado, to receive the first Aspen Award of $30,000 for service to the humanities. At the ceremony, he expressed his belief in music that might 'speak to or for' people, of the dangers of pressurising artists to produce proletarian music or to practise 'the latest *avant-garde* tricks', and of the economic difficulties faced by most musicians. He made cautionary comments on the recording and mass communication of music, believing these to be no substitute for the experience of live music-making in which each performance differently re-creates an original work. In October, he was further honoured by receiving the Royal Philharmonic Society's Gold Medal. In the same month, he and the English Opera Group travelled to the Soviet Union for performances of his three chamber operas, *The Rape of Lucretia*, *Albert Herring* and *The Turn of the Screw*.

For 1965, Peter Pears had organised for himself a near-complete sabbatical, free from routine engagements (save the Aldeburgh Festival), and, in January, he, Britten and the Hesses began a six-week holiday in India, where Britten began work on his *Gemini Variations*. In April he completed a new song cycle for the German baritone Dietrich Fischer-Dieskau, *Songs and Proverbs of William Blake*, which was to have its première at that year's Festival, with the composer playing the piano: according to the Britten scholar Peter Evans, this powerful work designed for the singer's world-weary yet compassionate voice offers 'resignation rather than resolution'. After the Festival, he directed a recording of *Curlew River* and then composed the choral work *Voices for Today*, commissioned for the 20th anniversary of the United Nations: its text, by writers of many eras and countries, have in common the theme of reconciliation and love between peoples and begin and end with Christ's admonition, 'If you have ears to hear, then hear!'. *Voices for Today* received simultaneous premières in New York, Paris and London on 24 October, and the UN's Secretary-General, U Thant, declared that 'To Benjamin Britten, the ideal of peace is a matter of personal and abiding concern...Today he speaks for all of us, with an eloquence we lack, in a medium of which he is a master.'

Britten and Pears in Armenia in August 1965.

Before this, there had been time for another holiday. Thanks to Rostropovich and his wife, this was in Dilizhan, Armenia, in a 'composers' village' in beautiful mountain scenery, where the party of four settled down to enjoy fine excursions and delicious food and drink. Pears was to write of one of these trips:

'The view was staggering...The air was superb; one breathed flowers and sun, and Ben and I climbed up higher still after our coffee, and somehow the whole world was explainable, so dizzy and beautiful it was...Today we ache...one's of Ben's toes is raw and in Elastoplast, and my knee, which was not good when I left London, is now *very* not good. However, it was a heavenly day.'

While here, Britten composed for 'Galya and Slava' a cycle of Pushkin songs set in the original Russian, *The Poet's Echo*, and the four friends also attended a Britten Festival in the Armenian capital, Yerevan. A visit to Pushkin's house and museum was another highlight of this holiday. So was a visit to Shostakovich, who was anxious to hear the new songs and, as a football fan, talked of attending the 1966 World Cup in England. Pears wrote a diary of this holiday that has since been published, and concluded, 'Never could any two guests have been more royally treated...we came back with much increased friendly feelings for these marvellous people.' He and Britten chose to value these human contacts without worrying too much about the Soviet political system, but knew that their friends belonged to an élite whose lifestyle bore scant resemblance to that of ordinary citizens of the Soviet Union.

Back in Aldeburgh, Britten composed his second church parable, *The Burning Fiery Furnace*, again with William Plomer as his librettist, as he was to be for the third, *The Prodigal Son*. This story of the three young Jews whose faith survives King Nebuchadnezzar's fire is more colourful than that of *Curlew River*, and the ensemble reflects this and includes a raucous trombone and a 'Babylonian drum'. The new piece had its première during the 1966 Aldeburgh Festival, in Orford Church like its predecessor (and its successor *The Prodigal Son*).

However, Britten's work on it had been interrupted in February, when he was operated on for an abdominal condition, diverticulitis. After this, he went to convalesce in Marrakesh, writing to tell Pears,

'I am sorry I have been such a drag on you these last years; with so much to think about, it has been wretched for you to have the extra worry of my tum. However, having today had the first taste of ease & efficiency in that quarter, I am determined that all this has not been in vain, & that you'll never have to give my health (or that part of my anatomy) another thought – !'

Later in 1966, Britten composed his 'vaudeville' short opera *The Golden Vanity* for the Vienna Boys' Choir. Set on board ship, it is not unlike a miniature *Billy Budd*, though the tone is far lighter. The heroic Cabin-boy saves his shipmates from the Turkish pirates, but his captain then allows him to drown rather than receive, as promised for his heroism, his daughter's hand. This lively piece was heard, and given an immediate complete encore, at the 1967 Aldeburgh Festival, which was unusually successful, with ticket sales at £44,000 nearly

Queen Elizabeth opening
The Maltings at Snape in
1967.

doubling those of the previous year. That year, the Queen
opened a magnificent new concert hall, The Maltings at Snape:
this had been a vast conversion and cost the Aldeburgh Festival
around £175,000, but seemed at once to justify itself. In
September, Britten and Pears again took the English Opera
Group to Canada for Montreal's Expo '67, after which they
gave a New York recital and embarked on a British Council tour
covering several Latin American countries. Here, as in the
Soviet Union, they became aware of the wide popularity of
Britten's music and of how highly regarded they were as
performers. At the end of the tour, in Rio de Janeiro, they saw
a production, in English, of *Peter Grimes*.

Early in 1968, Britten again rented his Venetian apartment
in the Palazzo Mocenigo in order to compose *The Prodigal Son*,
working in the morning and, in the afternoons, wandering into
the city's churches. Seemingly, he was glad to get away from
Aldeburgh, where he felt increasingly weighed down by his
Festival and English Opera Group responsibilities. Furthermore,
according to Imogen Holst, he had now 'reached the stage of self-
criticism as a composer when each new work was proving increasingly
difficult to write...he wanted "to think more and more about less and
less".' *The Prodigal Son* received its première in the 1968
Aldeburgh Festival.

Later that summer, Britten participated in an Edinburgh Festival featuring his music and Schubert's, during which Pears and he performed *Die Winterreise* (on 20 August). This was a happy stroke of planning, for Schubert was an especial favourite of his, and he once admitted to dreaming of meeting him in Vienna and that this dream had 'blessed the following days' [1].

During these three weeks, Britten, Pears, Rostropovich and Vishnevskaya (both of whom were performing his music) shared the same rented house with Donald Mitchell and his wife Kathleen, and she remembers that they were all 'stunned and bewildered' when on 21 August the Russian army invaded Czechoslovakia to crush its increasingly liberal régime. Even so, the composer likened Russia's grip on her satellite to the American presence on air bases in Britain, and preferred not to sign a telegram of protest drafted by the Czech conductor Rafael Kubelik, condemning the Soviet Union's action but believing in maintaining individual links which might ultimately change her policy.

In February 1969, Britten conducted a television recording of *Peter Grimes*, made at his insistence in The Maltings rather than a London studio: Pears sang the title role and Heather Harper was Ellen. But in the meantime, disaster struck the Aldeburgh Festival when The Maltings had a major fire during the night of 7–8 June. In this crisis Britten showed a surprising calm and the Festival went ahead as planned, with the stage production of Mozart's *Idomeneo* successfully transferred to Blythburgh Church. Fortunately, insurance covered rebuilding and some minor improvements, and in October Britten and Pears gave recitals in New York and Boston to help finance this work; the composer also gave his £10,000 fee for *Owen Wingrave*, an opera commissioned for BBC television. The new hall, which cost £225,000, was to be ready in time for the Queen to open the 1970 Festival, and it was announced that it now had 'expensive sprinklers whose efficiency we hope we shall never have to put to the test, but which are not designed to cool off musical enthusiasm'.

These were years in which Briten composed some sombre pieces, *Owen Wingrave* being among them. His heart-rending *Children's Crusade* for boys' choir, keyboards and percussion is to a text by Bertolt Brecht describing the wanderings and final disappearance of a group of children in war-torn Poland; so rhythmically free is it that he had difficulty in writing it down.

After the Maltings fire, he wrote his song cycle *Who are these children?*, to poems by the Scotsman William Soutar. Some of them are in dialect, and the last, called 'The Auld Aik', tells how a great oak has been felled and ends with the repeated word 'doun, doun'. 'It really *is* down, you see', Britten was to say, 'it's the end of everything'. The same pessimism informs the preceding poem, 'The Children', which seems to depict the aftermath of an air raid with the line, 'The blood of children stares from the broken stone'. In America later that year, interviewed by the *New York Times* and asked about his sympathy with the young, he replied:

'I try to avoid giving that kind of thing any thought...I do know that violence worries me. I become frightfully angry when children are treated badly. Maybe there is something in my subconscious that gives rise to this and I am suppressing it.'

In 1970, increasingly needing to escape from Aldeburgh's administrative pressures and the sound of aircraft from the nearby American air base at Bentwaters, Britten bought and improved a cottage about 20 miles distant to which he could retreat to work undisturbed. This was Chapel House at Horham, and the address was kept private; he had there a calm view over fields that offered space and silence. 'Night and silence – these are two of the things I cherish most', he once said. But he still travelled that spring with the English Opera Group to Australia and, with Pears, gave recitals there and in New Zealand that were followed by a ten-day holiday. At Alice Springs, in the crystal-clear light of the central desert, he and

The Chapel House at Horham.

115

the Australian painter Sydney Nolan watched a group of Aboriginal boys walking across the landscape. Later they discussed the idea of a ballet that would somehow contrast the freedom of an Aboriginal childhood with the constraints imposed on western children, though this project went no further.

That August, Britten completed *Owen Wingrave*. Based on a story by Henry James, the opera tells of a young man of military family whose heroic pacifism in the face of pressures from his relatives and fiancée costs him his life, and the composer could identify with Owen, whose stated creed in Act 2 ('Peace is not silent, it is the voice of love') reflected his own beliefs. As with his earlier James opera, *The Turn of the Screw*, his librettist was Myfanwy Piper, and the opera was first shown on BBC television in May 1971. Later, in May 1973, it was staged at Covent Garden. But Britten was not present, as three days before he had undergone major heart surgery.

These were years of increasing health troubles. In 1968 Britten had been hospitalised for a month for sub-acute endocarditis (a heart infection) and, from 1970 onwards, he experienced a lassitude that handicapped and depressed him. According to Imogen Holst, people were 'distressed to see how white and drawn he looked' after conducting Mozart's *Requiem* at the 1971 Aldeburgh Festival. Things there had become difficult and the Festival manager Stephen Reiss, who had held his post for 15 years and was the dedicatee of *A Midsummer Night's Dream*, had resigned after increasing tensions. Even so, during that year Britten wrote his *Third Suite for Cello* for Rostropovich, was again in the Soviet Union for a British Music Week, and recorded Bach's *St John Passion* and Elgar's *The Dream of Gerontius*, with Pears as the tenor soloist.

An autograph manuscript page from *Death in Venice*.

In October 1971, Britten travelled to Venice with Pears and the Pipers. This was partly to steep himself in the city's atmosphere, for he had already asked Mrs Piper if she would write the libretto for a new opera based on Thomas Mann's novella *Death in Venice*. Her initial reaction was to think the task impossible, but the second was that 'if Britten said so, it could be done.' The story is of a middle-aged, eminent writer, Aschenbach, dissatisfied with his work and holidaying alone in Venice. There he becomes obsessed with a young Polish boy, Tadzio, in whom he sees the embodiment of a beauty which is real and no mere artist's creation; but he cannot bring himself

Peter Pears in the role of
Aschenbach in the opera
Death in Venice.

to speak to him. Increasingly troubled, and then discovering that the city is plague-stricken, Aschenbach stays on and dies strangely fulfilled. In this context, Britten himself must sometimes have felt, as another Mann character does in *Tonio Kröger*, 'sick to death of having to represent what is human without having myself a share in it', and may have agreed with Nietzsche that an artist was 'forever shut off from reality [yet longed] to venture into the most forbidden territory.' Given his own lifelong attraction to young boys, *Death in Venice* is surely the most revealingly personal of his operas – just as it was his last.[2] Peter Pears, for whom the role of Aschenbach was composed, was later to say:

'Aschenbach asks...what it is he has spent his life searching for. Knowledge? A lost innocence? And must the pursuit of beauty, of love, lead only to chaos? All questions Ben constantly asked himself.'

On 22 September 1972, at The Maltings, Britten and Pears gave what was to be their last recital in Britain. For Britten's doctor Ian Tait now found clear signs of cardiac deterioration and advised surgery. The composer now felt unwell and was unable to go upstairs without stopping. However, he was determined to finish *Death in Venice* and managed to complete the vocal score in December and the full score in March 1973. Later he said,

'I wanted passionately to finish this piece before anything happened. For one thing, it is probably Peter's last major operatic part; for another, it was an opera I had been thinking about for a very long time...I had to keep going, and then, when I had finished, put myself into the doctor's hands.'

The composer with Rita
Thomson at The Red House
in June, 1976.

After seeing a specialist, Britten was admitted to the London Clinic, and then entered the National Heart Hospital for intensive medication followed by catheterisation. It was then decided that a valve replacement was needed. His operation on 7 May lasted about six hours, and he suffered a slight stroke – possibly because some particle of matter escaped the filters and lodged in his brain – which affected his right side. Later, too, it was found that the operation had partly failed: the enlarged heart did not return to its normal size and it became clear to Dr Tait that the likelihood of the composer's returning to reasonable health was 'very doubtful...a great disappointment, I never felt able to discuss this with him openly.' When Britten returned home later in May, he was accompanied at his request by Rita Thomson, a nurse from the National Heart Hospital. She stayed with him in Suffolk for a few days, and thereafter Britten kept in touch with her.

Britten never again played or conducted in public, and could not attend the première of *Death in Venice*, which the young conductor Steuart Bedford directed on 16 June 1973 at The Maltings. But although depressed, he gradually came to feel a little better and attended a Covent Garden performance of the opera on 18 October. Its critical reception was warm, with rapturous praise for Pears's performance as Aschenbach: in *The Guardian*, Edward Greenfield saluted 'one of the richest and deepest of operatic character-studies'.

During the second half of 1973, Britten spent much time recuperating at Horham, but in October he went with Pears on a motoring holiday in Wales and told Myfanwy Piper, 'Peter looks after me like a saint.' He took no part in the public celebration of his 60th birthday that November, which was marked by an all-Britten day on the BBC's Radio 3 and an Albert Hall concert. The Aldeburgh Festival's manager Bill Servaes, with his wife, took him out one evening and found him 'in the depths of depression, saying, "When's it all going to get better?"' But in the following spring Rita Thomson joined his household as a living-in nurse and a change in medication brought an improvement in his condition. After the 1974 Festival, in which excerpts from *Paul Bunyan* were performed, he decided to look at the work again and make some revisions; two years later it was to be staged at Aldeburgh with considerable success.

In the summer of 1974, Britten recommenced composition with his *Canticle V*, *The Death of Saint Narcissus*, a setting of an enigmatic poem by T.S. Eliot. By the end of the year, he was able to tell Alan Blyth of *The Times*:

'I suddenly got my confidence back about five months ago, and now composing has become, apart from anything else, a marvellous therapy. Now that I can write again, I have the feeling of being some use once more.'

Another new work, completed that November, was his surprisingly stark and moving *Suite on English Folk Tunes*, subtitled *'A time there was...'*: 'good I hope', he wrote to Pears, who was in the New York Metropolitan Opera's production of *Death in Venice.* [3] This letter was also a remarkable declaration of love: 'What *have* I done to deserve such an artist and *man* to write for? ...I love you—', and Pears's reply was no less heartfelt: 'No one has ever had a lovelier letter...But you know, Love is blind – and what your dear eyes do not see is that it is *you* who have given *me* everything, right from the beginning...And I can never be thankful enough to you and to Fate for all the heavenly joy we have had together for 35 years. My darling, I love you–'

None the less, their remarkable relationship had changed, and not only because they could no longer make music together. Although now 64 and no longer in perfect health, Pears was still in demand as a singer and teacher and showed no wish to retire. Indeed, he was no more than a visitor to the Red House and Horham save during Festival time, and recognized that Rita Thomson was in more immediate touch with his friend. Humphrey Carpenter suggests in his biography that the composer may have partly reverted to a schoolboy role with the competent, kindly Rita as his matron, particularly in view of her description of him as 'the best brought-up little boy you could imagine'. In 1975 Pears wrote from America to tell Peg Hesse that Britten had not 'mentioned lately my coming back for a visit and he seems to have accepted my being away until Christmas. I must say that the thought of such a visit appals me. I have been on the same pills as Ben, still am. My heartbeat is much too irregular (always was!) and my blood pressure much too high'.

During 1975 Britten composed two more works for Pears, one being *Sacred and Profane*, for the Wilbye Consort, a vocal ensemble which Pears directed, and the other a splendidly vigorous Burns cycle for voice and harp called *A Birthday Hansel*, commissioned by the Queen for her mother's 75th birthday. For that year's Aldeburgh Festival and the mezzo Janet Baker, he wrote a passionately dramatic solo cantata *Phaedra*, on words from Racine's play, portraying the lustful, guilty Athenian queen who takes poison and, as the cantata ends, sings, 'My eyes at last give up their light, and see the day they've soiled resume its purity.' Although now using a wheelchair, he travelled that November to Venice with Rita Thomson and Bill and Pat Servaes. There, in his suite at the Hotel Danieli, he completed his *Third String Quartet*, which quotes from *Death in Venice* and has a slow final movement subtitled 'La Serenissima' (an old name for the city). The work has a mysterious glowing beauty which was new in his music: its first performance was to take place shortly after his death.

Britten and Pears enjoying a garden party at The Red House in 1976.

Britten photographed on the 24th of September 1976, shortly before he died.

Throughout 1976, Britten's homograft heart valve of human tissue deteriorated and he experienced a progressive heart failure. In March he made a new will, telling his solicitor, Isador Caplan, that Pears's future was 'far more important to me than anything that is going on at Aldeburgh, or anything to do with my music'; his executors and trustees were to be Pears, Caplan, his accountant Leslie Periton and Donald Mitchell. Britten also asked Mitchell to write a book about him and his music, saying, 'I want you to tell the truth about Peter and me.' Later, Pears was to say that Britten became glad in these years to see an increasing British tolerance of homosexuality, although 'the word "gay" was not in his vocabulary'. In June, the composer was created a life peer. There was a celebratory garden party at the Red House, and a touching picture exists of Pears pushing Britten's wheelchair back to the house as the guests departed: Kathleen Mitchell describes this as 'a joyful occasion on a wonderful day. Nothing elegiac about it'. That June, the composer attended some Aldeburgh Festival performances, including the revival of *Paul Bunyan*. After that, escaping the exceptionally hot English summer, he went on holiday to Norway with Pears and Rita Thomson.

Britten now completed the vocal score of one more composition, a five-movement *Welcome Ode* for local schools to perform for the Queen's jubilee visit in the following year. However, he left the writing-out of the orchestration to the young composer Colin Matthews, now assisting him. He then commenced work on a cantata to an Edith Sitwell text, *Praise we great men*, but this was to remain unfinished. In September he heard the Amadeus Quartet play through his *Third Quartet*, and in October he attended a cabaret evening in Aldeburgh's Jubilee Hall at which Peter Pears sang Noël Coward's 'I'll see you again'. This was to be Britten's last public appearance. Two ladies who were present felt that the tenor really meant the farewell in it to be Ben's. And Rita was wiping the sweat off Ben's face. At the end, when there was a toast to 'The next 30 years', Ben got to his feet and drained his glass right to the bottom, and stepped out of sight, and that was the last time we ever saw him.

Soon after this, Britten took to his bed. Peter Pears had again crossed the Atlantic to perform and teach, but in November Rita Thomson informed him that his friend's condition had worsened and he returned in haste. Later, he was to say, 'I shouldn't really have gone', but his presence cheered Britten who for a while seemed to improve and gave a small champagne party on his birthday, the 22nd; among the guests who came briefly to see him in his bedroom were his two sisters and Peg Hesse. But it was clear that his illness was terminal and the Bishop of Ipswich brought him Holy Communion. According to Pears, he was 'direct and unafraid' at the prospect of dying:

'we'd faced up to what was going to come a good deal earlier than this...But what was his greatest feeling was sadness and sorrow at the thought of leaving me, and his friends and his responsibilities. That was what occupied him more than anything else. He'd always said earlier to me, 'I must die first, because I don't know what I'd do without you.''

During the early hours of 4 December, Britten's breathing deteriorated and Rita Thomson called Pears to his bedside. Pears said later, 'He died in my arms, in fact, peacefully... there was no struggle to keep alive, except the purely physical one, which one can't help, to breathe.' In a letter, he wrote, 'His hand was in mine.' The Queen sent him a private message of sympathy, of which he said, 'It's a recognition of the way we lived.' Three days later, Britten's funeral took place at Aldeburgh Parish Church, and the Bishop of Ipswich gave an address ending with the words, 'Ben will like the sound of the trumpets, although he will find it difficult to believe they are sounding for him.' The composer's family and closest friends then attended the burial, in a grave lined with rushes from the Snape marshes.

(1) Other favourites, whom he named in a 1960s interview, were Mozart, Purcell, Bach, Verdi, Tchaikovsky, Mahler and Berg. One notes the absence of Beethoven and Wagner, and any of the French composers. However, he admired Debussy (a diary entry in 1932 refers to his 'incomparable' orchestral *Nocturnes*) and occasionally took part in performances of his music, including a recording of the *Cello Sonata* with Rostropovich and an Aldeburgh Festival *En blanc et noir* with Sviatoslav Richter.

(2) When writing his *Benjamin Britten* (Faber and Faber, 1992), Humphrey Carpenter interviewed several men to whom, as boys, Britten was attracted. Most were aware of his affection, but regarded it as more fatherly than lustful, and in no case do we have an account of a sexual incident.

(3) This subtitle is that of the sombre final song in *Winter Words*, which ends with the reiterated question, 'How long?'

Chapter 9

'A time there was...'

Britten's final resting place in the churchyard of Aldeburgh Parish Church.

Britten once said that he 'had a very strong feeling that people died at the right moment', and the valedictory note is clear in much of his last music from *Death in Venice* onwards. Martin Lovett of the Amadeus Quartet thought the *Third Quartet* a swan song, and the critic Bayan Northcott noted its 'final page of touchingly heaven-inspired textures, complemented at the very end by a deep, almost Mahlerian sigh.' Yet is is misleading to paint so simple a picture. Less of a romantic than Mahler, and with an English upbringing that saved him from self-pity, he had faced death with some stoicism. Admittedly, there was an unknown to face, but he did this without terror. In some moods he may even have felt like Wilfred Owen's soldier in the *War Requiem* ('we've walked quite friendly up to Death; Sat down and eaten with him, cool and bland'), though he could not share the faith of St Nicolas ('Lord, I come to life, to final birth').

The composer with Yehudi Menuhin rehearsing for the 1958 Aldeburgh Festival.

Warned of Britten's condition, the press had its obituaries ready. In the *Sunday Times*, Desmond Shawe-Taylor declared that he had earned 'not only respect for a long series of fine achievements but something akin to love...he enriched the failing store of happiness.' In the *Sunday Telegraph*, Bayan Northcott noted the atmospheric quality of his music, 'those shining, darkly bright lines and textures that could evoke a bleak sea coast or a magical nightscape so completely.' Musicians also paid tributes: Malcolm Williamson, the Master of the Queen's Music, said, 'Benjamin Britten preached peace through his music. We wish him the peace for which he strove in this world', and Michael Tippett called him 'the most musical person I have ever met...Dear, dear Ben, to the end I keep a place warm in my heart.' Yehudi Menuhin mentioned his 'eternal youthfulness [which] accounts for his identification with young people...he was greatly loved, like Orpheus.' Others offered more qualified praise. In the *Observer*, Peter Heyworth referred to Britten's 'unchallenged position in the public mind as the leading British composer of his time' and thus

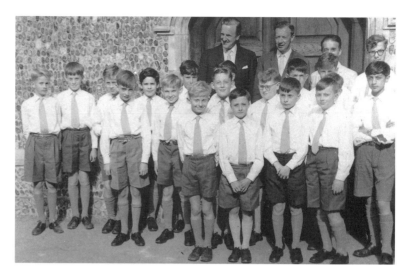

Britten and Pears with the London Boys Singers at the 1962 Aldeburgh Festival.

managed to imply that he himself might think otherwise, while the *Daily Telegraph's* Martin Cooper praised his brilliance but also noted his 'emotional immaturity'. However, the *Telegraph's* formal obituary called Britten 'the truly towering talent of his age' and stated that for the first time in 300 years England had produced a great composer. In *The Times*, a notice running to eighty column inches called Britten 'much more than the leading English composer of his time':

'He was a high-minded and high-principled person [and] his absolute honesty was dictated by his faith, as was his contempt for power and violence. His early left-wing socialism remained with him as a moral and social, rather than dogmatically political, belief...rarely have such artistic endowments been matched with such a sense of human responsibility for their best use.'

A leading article in the same paper, headed 'A Dedicated Life', resumed this theme and added:

'For the countryman nature was a constant inspiration, especially the sea; for the Christian pacifist there were sacred music, hatred of cruelty and all oppression; above all compassion for the victim and the nonconformist, and constant exploration into the world of childhood. Those themes often meet and collide in his works memorably, in *Billy Budd* and the *Children's Crusade* and *Death in Venice*.'

A few days later, again in *The Times*, the poet Geoffrey Grigson wrote, more personally, of Britten's kindness remaining 'incandescent in memory':

124

'If you encountered personal kindness from this great man, you encountered what was also an element in the piercing benediction of his music. This kindness was sympathy, not condescension, a portion of that total sympathy with man and child, with existence and sentience, which made him, for instance, find the poetry he involed in his music...I know that this Christmas many, many homes will play the record of *A Ceremony of Carols* with a mixed infinity of pleasure, thanks and tears.'

These tributes went on for some weeks. The Performing Right Society's journal called Britten 'an illustrious example of that still very rare phenomenon, a creator of unmistakable, authentic genius', and in *Opera*, Sir Georg Solti used the same word, adding, 'his departure has left an enormous emptiness'.

Several Britten anecdotes also appeared, and though these 'human interest' stories may seem journalistic, they accord with his musical personality, for here, too, we find the instant sympathy, the practicality and the mischievous humour. Ernest Bradbury, of the *Yorkshire Post*, remembered his two children spotting Britten and Pears in a concert audience and asking for their autographs:

'As, obligingly as ever, they were signing, I went up behind and said: 'You probably wouldn't do that if you knew their father was a critic.' Said Ben promptly, with that marvellous screwed-up smile, 'There are critics and critics!' I can't remember what I heard after that, but I'm sure it got a good notice.

'And of course, Britten, too, could be critical, though never in an academic way. I remember him showing me a passage in Sibelius's *Sixth Symphony* and saying, 'I think he must have been drunk when he wrote that!'.'

A good account of Britten at home came from the record producer John Culshaw, writing in the magazine *Gramophone*:

'The Red House really was peace: a large rambling place secluded from the town, to which various extensions and conversions had been added over the years. To be a weekend guest there was to relax completely; although, before his illness, Ben's own ideas about relaxation might not totally coincide with those of a city-dweller. Of course nothing was obligatory, and I enjoyed the long country walks, not least because he was an expert ornithologist, whereas I cannot tell a curlew from a duck; but I confess that more often than not I dodged

The composer enjoying a game of tennis as a younger man.

the early morning swim before breakfast because, as a city-dweller, I had been awakened hours earlier by the dawn chorus of birds which those who live regularly in the country never seem to hear. By the time the birds had shut up I would be fast asleep again, and Ben and Peter would be in the pool or walking the dogs in the garden or at breakfast.

'One of the cruellest ironies of Ben's early death is that he had kept himself so fit. He was no kind of health fanatic, but until the final illess he enjoyed the outdoor life: he walked regularly, he swam, he played tennis. He did not smoke, but he enjoyed a drink if there was conversation to go with it. He loved good food, and the best food of all was at The Red House because it was fresh, like fish straight out of the sea with vegetables from the garden. The last time we had a meal together at The Red House,...we had grilled sprats which, he remarked, 'really are worth the awful smell they make in the kitchen'. Maybe it seems trivial to mention such things, but I don't think so, because they show the other side of a shy public figure. However well-read, however sensitive, however concerned about the state of music and indeed the state of man, he was at heart, like Elgar with whose music he eventually came to terms, a countryman. A deceptive simplicity, an earthiness, lies behind all his music, just as it does behind the music of his beloved Schubert.'

A service of thanksgiving for Benjamin Britten was held on 10 March 1977 in Westminster Abbey. The Queen Mother and many other public figures attended, and the Dean of Westminster spoke of

'the concern and eagerness with which he entered into life's joys and sorrows, and out of which his music was begotten and born...We remember him as a composer, who by the purity of his vision and dedicated use of exceptional powers inspired both young and old to find fulfilment in making music. We think of him as the interpreter of his generation in its recoil from the horrors of war and its determination to advance a world of justice, peace and human brotherhood.'

At this service, Peter Pears read the Abraham and Isaac story from Genesis, which inspired Britten's second canticle and recurs in his *War Requiem*. The congregation sang the two hymns from *Saint Nicolas* and a chamber group played the slow movement of Schubert's *String Quintet*. In the address, Walter Hussey, now the Dean of Chichester, called the composer less an orthodox churchman than 'a person of deeply thoughtful moral character'. He added that, despite his success, 'he was also a man who knew sorrow and disappointment...Perhaps because of his sensitive nature he felt it especially deeply, but joy and happiness kept breaking through and finding expression in his music. Although there was nothing whatsoever childish about him, his nature was child-like, complex and simple.'

Britten and Pears at Snape in 1974.

In 1978, Peter Pears was knighted for his services to music, and went again to Westminster Abbey for the unveiling and dedication of a Britten memorial stone. Sir Lennox Berkeley was also there, and a third old friend, Wystan Auden, was also represented when Pears read his poem 'The Composer':

All the others translate: the painter sketches
A visible world to love or reject;
Rummaging into his living, the poet fetches
The images out that hurt and connect,

From Life to Art by painstaking adaption,
Relying on us to uncover the rift;
Only your notes are pure contraption,
Only your song is an absolute gift.

Pour out your presence, a delight cascading
The falls of the knee and the weirs of the spine,
Our climate of silence and doubt invading;

You alone, alone, imaginary song,
Are unable to say an existence is wrong,
And pour out your forgiveness like a wine.

Another memorial to Britten was the Britten-Pears School for Advanced Musical Studies at the Snape Maltings. Founded earlier in the decade, this had been helped by his 'charitable fund' bequest of £100,000. Together with the Aldeburgh Festival and the Britten-Pears Library at the Red House, they have given a permanent sense of place to his work. As for his manuscript scores, some now belong to the British Library in settlement of capital transfer tax, but remain on permanent loan in the Britten-Pears Library.

As 1976 receded, it became clear that the interest in Britten's music, and in the man himself, remained lively. Several new recordings of his music appeared and 1980 saw the broadcasting of three hour-long documentary radio programmes compiled by Donald Mitchell. The subject of his sexuality had been publicly aired for the first time in 1977 when, in the *Musical Times*, Philip Brett argued that *Peter Grimes* was the composer's apologia for his way of life. The matter was further discussed by Donald Mitchell and Hans Keller in a further BBC talk called 'Britten in retrospect', but they disagreed as to its relevance to his music, Keller thinking it more important than Mitchell. In the same year came Tony Palmer's two-hour TV documentary *A time there was...*. With Donald Mitchell's collaboration, Palmer achieved balance and perspective, and Sir Peter Pears spoke with memorable sincerity. As Sean Day-Lewis wrote in the *Daily Telegraph*, here were Britten's familiar adult features, ascetic and mourning lost innocence...

'from the moment when we were reminded of that marvellous transfixing moment when Pears sings of the Great Bear in *Peter Grimes* to the final memories of the life-saving nurse Rita Thomson, who made Britten's last compositions possible, tears were never far from my eyes.'[1]

And so, it might seem, the tale has been told. Yet, as one obituarist wrote, we need not write of Britten in the past tense when he is 'all future'. His foundation of an opera company, a festival with its concert hall, and a school of music reminds us of his feeling for historical continuity. Though never an intellectually motivated innovator like Schönberg, he made real and purposeful innovations. Among these was his establishment of an operatic form relying neither on the classical 'set piece' technique nor on Wagnerian through-composition: his approach was more flexible than either. His writing for chamber orchestras created a new sound in British music, and he extended the technical and expressive range of

Peter Pears teaching the soprano Lynn Dawson at the Britten-Pears School for Advanced Musical Studies in 1979.

instruments like the harp, guitar, cello and percussion. He also adapted to western musical terms, as early as *Paul Bunyan* but principally in his later music, the subtle oriental technique of heterophony, once defined as simultaneously offering 'several layers of elaboration' on a melodic line or even a kind of semi-unison. He left a whole pioneering repertory of children's pieces, from *Friday Afternoons* to the *Welcome Ode*; without his example it is impossible to imagine the many that have been written since, like Sir Peter Maxwell Davies' *Kirkwall Shopping Songs*. The musicals of Andrew Lloyd Webber and Tim Rice, with their flawed or lonely protagonists, also owe something to his choice of subject matter.

The ability to integrate and reconcile opposites is the musical side to Britten's pacifism. He incorporated into his work jazz, oriental idioms and English hymn tunes, and sometimes invited his audience to perform. The past and present were part of his continuum, so that Dowland and Purcell could, as it were, become his collaborators, while children and adults combine to give a unique human depth to works as different as *A Midsummer Night's Dream* and the *War Requiem*.

Some people accuse Britten of emotional immaturity. Yet much of his music is wholly adult, and *Death in Venice*, *The Turn of the Screw* and *Peter Grimes* discuss the perennial failure of adults to communicate with children. We should never overlook the joyful affirmation of *A Ceremony of Carols*, *The Young Person's Guide to the Orchestra*, *Albert Herring*, *Saint Nicolas*, the *Spring*

129

Symphony and the *Cantata Academica*. Apart from *Albert Herring*, how many comic operas have been written in the 20th century? And its happy love music for Sid and Nancy is no less unambiguously heterosexual than the musical depiction of Tarquinius's lust in *The Rape of Lucretia*.

Far from sitting in a proverbial ivory tower, Britten used all of today's instruments of mass communication. He was a radio performer from the 1930s, composed important film and radio scores in a perfect apprenticeship for writing opera, and, in *Owen Wingrave*, created an opera for television. Despite his Aspen Award reservations about recorded music ('not part of true musical experience...a substitute, and dangerous because deluding'), this composer made fuller use of the recording studio than any contemporary. As a pianist, he recorded about 40 works, and as a conductor, more still; there is even a recording from 1946 in which he played the viola in Purcell's *Fantasia upon one note* [2] Many of these recorded performances are outstanding, for he brought a composer's insight to other music beside his own.

Though meticulous and exacting with orchestras and choirs, Britten did not much enjoy rehearsing and was easily wearied by retakes during recording sessions. Rehearsing with Pears as a duo was another matter altogether, because of their extraordinary rapport: the tenor told a colleague that they spoke little but, where something could be improved, simply stopped and went back, sometimes without a word. This rapport led them to be called one of the greatest of musical partnerships. Donald Mitchell has described one piano-less 'rehearsal' of a tricky song by Percy Grainger that took place during a flight from New York to Boston: Britten's strong, slender fingers tapped on his briefcase while Pears, beside him, sang almost inaudibly, and next day, in their recital, the song went perfectly.

Britten's music appeals strongly to young and old, as performers and listeners, when people are often alienated by new pieces that seem to them meaningless, ugly or at the other extreme crudely popular. Without compromising his standards, this composer wrote 'for human beings – directly and deliberately...to be of use to people, to please them, to "enhance their lives".' His success in reaching people of different ages, cultures, and political or religious views remains unique among composers of his generation, and maybe even of his century.

Benjamin Britten 1913-1976.

Traditionally, time is the arbiter of an artist's work, determining whether it will achieve classic status. In Britten's case, it has already done so, since his music is regularly heard in concert halls, opera houses, churches and schools. Its survival seems beyond reasonable doubt. If we ask why, we may conclude that its remarkable skill is demonstrable, at least by musicians to musicians; more importantly, its humanity enriches our lives.

[1] This reference is to the 'horoscope' aria, when Grimes meditates on his fate in the words, 'Who can turn skies back and begin again?'.

[2] He chose this work for the final side of a recording of his *Second String Quartet*. He played only the sustained note, a middle C, and a colleague remembers him as being 'terribly nervous'.

Catalogue of works

This list gives only the works to which Britten allocated opus numbers. However, he also wrote a mass of juvenalia and incidental music for theatre, film and radio, and since his death a number of youthful compositions have been published, performed and recorded. There are also numerous arrangements, mainly of British folk songs. For a complete catalogue, see the Britten Estate's publication *A Britten Source Book*. Three works listed here (Op. 16, 17 and 39) were withdrawn by the composer, although he revised *Paul Bunyan* in 1974 for a new production.

Op. 1   *Sinfonietta*, chamber orchestra, 1932
2   *Phantasy*, oboe and string trio, 1932
3   *A Boy was Born*, mixed voices, 1933
4   *Simple Symphony*, strings, 1934
5   *Holiday Diary*, piano, 1934
6   *Suite*, violin and piano, 1935
7   *Friday Afternoons*, children's voices and piano, 1935
8   *Our Hunting Fathers*, high voice and orchestra, 1936
9   *Soirées Musicales* (Rossini arr. Britten), orchestra, 1936
10   *Variations on a Theme of Frank Bridge*, strings, 1937
11   *On This Island*, high voice and piano, 1937
12   *Mont Juic* (with Lennox Berkeley), orchestra, 1937
13   *Piano Concerto*, piano and orchestra, 1938
14   *Ballad of Heroes*, voices and orchestra, 1939
15   *Violin Concerto*, violin and orchestra, 1939
16   *Young Apollo*, piano and strings, 1939
17   *Paul Bunyan*, operetta, 1941
18   *Les Illuminations*, high voice and strings, 1939
19   *Canadian Carnival*, orchestra, 1939
20   *Sinfonia da Requiem*, orchestra, 1940
21   *Diversions*, piano (left hand) and orchestra, 1940
22   *Seven Sonnets of Michelangelo*, tenor and piano, 1940
23/1 *Introduction and Rondo alla Burlesca*, two pianos
23/2 *Mazurka Elegiaca*, two pianos, 1941
24   *Matinées Musicales* (Rossini arr. Britten), orchestra, 1941
25   *String Quartet No. 1 in D*, 1941
26   *Scottish Ballad*, two pianos and orchestra, 1941
27   *Hymn to St Cecilia*, mixed voices, 1942
28   *A Ceremony of Carols*, treble voices and harp, 1942

29	*Prelude and Fugue*, strings, 1943
30	*Rejoice in the Lamb*, voices and organ, 1943
31	*Serenade*, tenor, horn and strings, 1943
32	*Festival Te Deum*, chorus and organ, 1944
33	*Peter Grimes*, opera, 1945
34	*The Young Person's Guide to the Orchestra*, orchestra 1946
35	*The Holy Sonnets of John Donne*, high voice and piano, 1945
36	*String Quartet No. 2 in C*, 1945
37	*The Rape of Lucretia*, opera, 1946
38	*Occasional Overture in C*, orchestra, 1946
39	*Albert Herring*, opera, 1947
40	*Canticle I*, high voice and piano, 1947
41	*A Charm of Lullabies*, mezzo-soprano and piano, 1947
42	*Saint Nicolas*, tenor, chorus and orchestra, 1948
43	*The Beggar's Opera* (realised by Britten from original), opera, 1948
44	*Spring Symphony*, solo voices, chorus and orchestra, 1949
45	*The Little Sweep*, children's opera, 1949
46	*A Wedding Anthem (Amo Ergo Sum)*, solo voices, chorus and organ, 1949
47	*Five Flower Songs*, mixed voices, 1950
48	*Lachrymae*, viola and piano, 1950
49	*Six metamorphoses after Ovid*, oboe, 1951
50	*Billy Budd*, opera, 1951
51	*Canticle II*, alto, tenor and piano, 1952
52	*Winter Words*, high voice and piano, 1953
53	*Gloriana*, opera, 1953
54	*The Turn of the Screw*, opera, 1954
55	*Canticle III*, tenor, horn and piano, 1954
56a	*Hymn to St Peter*, choir and organ, 1955
56b	*Antiphon*, choir and organ, 1956
57	*The Prince of the Pagodas*, ballet, 1956
58	*Songs from the Chinese*, high voice and guitar, 1957
59	*Noye's Fludde*, children's opera, 1957
60	*Nocturne*, tenor, seven instrumental soloists and chamber orchestra, 1958
61	*Sechs Hölderlin-Fragmente*, voice and piano, 1958
62	*Cantata Academica*, solo voices, chorus and orchestra, 1959
63	*Missa Brevis in D*, boys' voices and organ, 1959
64	*A Midsummer Night's Dream*, opera, 1960
65	*Sonata in C*, cello and piano, 1961
66	*War Requiem*, solo voices, choirs, organ and orchestra, 1961

67	*Psalm 150*, children's voices and instruments, 1962
68	*Symphony for Violoncello and Orchestra (Cello Symphony)*, 1963
69	*Cantata Misericordium*, solo voices, chorus and orchestra, 1963
70	*Nocturnal after John Dowland*, guitar, 1963
71	*Curlew River*, parable for church performance, 1964
72	*Suite for Cello (No.1)*, 1964
73	*Gemini Variations*, 'quartet for two players', 1965
74	*Songs and Proverbs of William Blake*, baritone and piano, 1965
75	*Voice for Today*, mixed chorus, 1965
76	*The Poet's Echo*, high voice and piano, 1965
77	*The Burning Fiery Furnace*, parable for church performance, 1966
78	*The Golden Vanity*, 'a vaudeville for boys and piano', 1966
79	*The Building of the House*, overture for orchestra and optional chorus, 1967
80	*Second Suite for Cello*, 1967
81	*The Prodigal Son*, parable for church performance, 1968
82	*Children's Crusade*, 'a ballad for children's voices and orchestra', 1968
83	*Suite for Harp*, 1969
84	*Who are these children?*, tenor and piano, 1969
85	*Owen Wingrave*, opera for television, 1970
86	*Canticle IV*, counter-tenor, tenor, baritone and piano, 1971
87	*Third Suite for Cello*, 1971
88	*Death in Venice*, opera, 1973
89	*Canticle V*, tenor and harp, 1974
90	*Suite on English Folk Tunes: 'A Time There Was...'*, orchestra, 1974
91	*Sacred and Profane*, for mixed voices, 1975
92	*A Birthday Hansel*, voice and harp, 1975
93	*Phaedra*, 'dramatic cantata for mezzo-soprano and small orchestra', 1975
94	*String Quartet No. 3*, 1975
95	*Welcome Ode*, young people's chorus and orchestra, 1976

Bibliography

Throughout his career, Britten attracted champions, and there are several published studies of his music. His personality has also fascinated authors. The books in this selected list have different virtues and will therefore appeal to different readers.

Benjamin Britten: A Biography, Humphrey Carpenter, Faber and Faber, 1992. The most compelling and comprehensive biography available, with penetrating if sometimes controversial comment.

Letter from a Life: Selected Letters and Diaries of Benjamin Britten 1913-76, Vols. 1 and 2, ed. Donald Mitchell and Philip Reed, Faber and Faber, 1991. Incomparably rich in material and commentary, although these first two volumes only take us as far as 1945.

Benjamin Britten: Pictures from a Life 1913-1976, Faber and Faber, 1978. A pictorial treatment unlikely to be surpassed.

On Receiving the First Aspen Award, Benjamin Britten, Faber and Faber, 1964. A brief but highly revealing credo from the composer.

The Music of Benjamin Britten, Peter Evans, J.M. Dent, revised edition 1989. A detailed scholarly commentary, but more useful to students than to the general reader.

Britten, Imogen Holst, Faber and Faber, third edition 1980. A thoughtful and well illustrated children's book.

Britten, Christopher Headington, Eyre Methuen, 1981. Although this was written before the availability of Britten's diaries and letters, I am proud to boast that Sir Peter Pears called it 'unquestionably the best book on Benjamin Britten'.

Britten, Michael Kennedy, J.M. Dent, 1981. Discusses both man and music in the publisher's Master Musicians series.

Remembering Britten, Alan Blyth, Hutchinson, 1981. Reminiscences by thirty people formerly close to the composer.

Peter Pears: A Biography, Christopher Headington, Faber and Faber, 1992. Contains much concerning the great tenor's lifelong partner.

Benjamin Britten: A Commentary on his works by a group of specialists, ed. Donald Mitchell and Hans Keller, Rockliff Publishing Corporation, 1952. After four decades, this pioneering work remains of interest for its early assessments.

Discography

Since fine Britten recordings abound, the only problem is choice. The 1996 *Gramophone Classical Good CD Guide* has nine pages devoted to his music, with a detailed critical recommendation of each disc or set which takes into account both performance and sound quality. The *Penguin Guide to Compact Discs and Cassettes* is also useful, and new editions frequently appear.

Further Reference

Felix Barker and Francis Jackson. **2000 Years Of London,** *London, 1974.*

Walter Besant. **Westminster,** *London, 1907.*

Jeremy Black and Jeremy Gregory (eds.). **Culture, Politics And Society In Britain 1660-1800,** *Manchester, 1991.*

Eric Blom. **Music In England,** *London, 1947 edition.*

Arthur Bryant. **Restoration England,** *London, 1960.*

E.J. Burford. **London, The Synfulle Citie,** *London, 1990.*

Sir George Clark. **The Later Stuarts 1660-1714,** *Oxford, 1932.*

Christopher Cook and John Wroughton. **English Historical Facts 1603-1688,** *London, 1980.*

W.H. Cummings. **Purcell,** *London, 1903.*

Arthur Dasent. **Nell Gwynne,** *London, 1924.*

Godfrey Davies. **The Early Stuarts 1603-1660,** *Oxford, 1959.*

Edward J. Dent. **Foundations Of English Opera,** *Cambridge, 1928.*

John Dryden. **Poems And Fables (ed. James Kinsley),** *Oxford, 1958.*

Maureen Duffy. **The Passionate Shepherdess, Aphra Behn, 1640-89,** *London, 1989 edition.*

Maureen Duffy. **Henry Purcell,** *London, 1994.*

Robert Elkin. **The Old Concert Rooms Of London,** *London, 1955.*

John Evelyn. **Diary (ed. William Bray, 1818), rev. edition,** *London, 1952.*

Antonia Fraser. **Charles II,** *London, 1993.*

Clement Antrobus Harris. **The Story Of British Music,** *London, c. 1920.*

John Harris, Stephen Orgel and Roy Strong. **The King's Arcadia: Inigo Jones And The Stuart Court,** *London, 1973.*

Geoffrey Holmes (ed.). **Britain After The Glorious Revolution 1689-1714,** *London, 1969.*

Imogen Holst (ed.). **Henry Purcell: Essays On His Music,** *London, 1959.*

Elizabeth Howe. **The First English Actresses: Women And Drama 1660-1700,** *Cambridge, 1992.*

Michael Hunter. **Science And Society In Restoration England,** *Cambridge, 1981.*

Arthur Hutchings. **Purcell,** *London, 1982.*

J.R. Jones. **The Revolution Of 1688 In England,** *London, 1972.*

J.R. Jones. **The Restored Monarchy 1660-1688,** *London, 1979.*

J.P. Kenyon. **The Stuarts,** *London, 1958.*

Robert King. **Henry Purcell,** *London, 1994.*

Robert Etheridge Moore. **Henry Purcell And The Restoration Theatre,** *London, 1961.*

Allardyce Nicoll. **British Drama (fifth edition),** *London, 1962.*

Roger North. **Essays On Music (ed. John Wilson),** *London, 1959.*

David Ogg. **England In The Reign Of Charles II,** *Oxford, 1956.*

Samuel Pepys. **Diary (ed. Lord Braybrooke, 1825),** *London, 1903.*

Curtis A. Price. **Henry Purcell And The London Stage,** *Cambridge, 1984.*

Sandra Richards. **The Rise Of The English Actress,** *London, 1993.*

David Thomas. **William Congreve,** *London, 1992.*

G.R.R. Treasure. **Seventeenth Century France,** *London, 1981.*

G.M. Trevelyan. **England Under The Stuarts, revised edition,** *London, 1925.*

Sir Jack Westrup. **Purcell,** *London, 1965.*

Franklin B. Zimmerman. **Henry Purcell,** *New York, 1967.*

Christopher Headington authored ten published books on music and contributed to many more: his earlier biography of Britten (1981), long out of print and completely rewritten for the present book, was described by Sir Peter Pears as 'the best book on Benjamin Britten that has yet appeared and is likely to remain so'. He was also a composer, a pianist with worldwide experience, and a teacher who was the Tutor in Music of the External Studies Department of Oxford University until becoming fully independent in 1982. As a composition student at the Royal Academy of Music in London, Christopher Headington was introduced to Benjamin Britten by his teacher Lennox Berkeley, and thereafter Britten gave him invaluable advice. His hobbies included flying light aircraft, skiing, travel and languages. Christopher Headington was tragically killed in a skiing accident in 1996, shortly before the publication of this volume.

Photo & Illustration Credits

(BPL) after an entry indicates print copied courtesy of The Britten-Pears Library.

B.W.Allen: 124(BPL); Erich Auerbach/Hulton Getty Collection: 60, 90, 104b,105; Alexander Bender/Hulton Getty Collection:45(BPL); BBC: 59t(BPL); Bodleian Library, Oxford:104t(BPL); Boosey & Hawkes: 32b, 40(both BPL); Benjamin Britten © The Britten-Pears Foundation: 19,24; Courtesy of The Britten-Pears Library: 1,2t,3t&b,4,5t&b,7,11,15,18,20t, 26,30t,32t, 33,35,36,47,48,68,80,89,94,95,109,110,111,123b,126; East Anglian Daily Times: 57b; Eastern Daily Press:113(BPL); Faber:116 (BPL); Fayer/Vienna: 82,ph.John Garner © Mrs J.Garner:117t(BPL); Bertl Gaye: 120b (BPL); ph.Kenneth Green © Gordon Green:49(BPL); Hulton Getty Collection: 97,101t,102; ph.Kurt Hutton © Peter Hutton: 42,72b, 73,76, 79,98,99,101b(all BPL); E.I.Iavno: 103(BPL); Lotte Jacobi Archives/ University of New Hampshire: 30b; Victor Kraft: 27(BPL); Nigel Luckhurst: 57t,120t,129; Angus McBean/Harvard Theatre Collection: 51L&r,59b(BPL),65,66; Denis de Marney/Hulton Getty Collection: 91;National Portrait Gallery: 2b(BPL),9t,56; Dr.W.Otto: 117b(BPL); Victor Parker: 127(BPL); ph.John Piper © Myfanwy Piper: 88(BPL); © The Post Office 1996 "the Post Office" is a registered trade mark of the Post Office. Reproduced by kind permission: 17; The Royal College of Music: 9b; Josef Sekal: 131(BPL); ph.Enid Slater © Bridget Kitley: 20b,22(both BPL); Rosamund Strode:123t(BPL); Clive Strutt: 72t,107(BPL); Rita Thomson: 115(BPL); Times Newspapers Limited, 1933: 13(BPL); Roger Wood: 83.

Index

References to illustrations are in **bold** type.
References to musical works, plays, magazines, newspapers etc are in *italic* type.
Almost invariably, references to Benjamin Britten can be cross-referenced with those to Peter Pears.

Abyssinia (Ethiopia) 18
Agra 94
Aldeburgh 21, 47, 67, 69, 73, 74, 76, 80, 83, 88, 93, 97, 101, 112, 113, 115, 118, 120, 121
Aldeburgh Festival 69, 75, 78, 83, 86, 89, 97, 98, 104, 109, 110, 111, 112, 113, 114, 116, 118, 119, 120, 122, 128
Aldeburgh Parish Church **73**, 121
Alice Springs 115
Alston, Audrey 5
Amadeus Quartet 76, 121, 123
America 25, 27ff
Amityville 29, 33
Ansermet, Ernest **60**, 60, 61
Antwerp 52
Aprahamian, Felix 92
Arts Council of Great Britain 42, 79
Aschenbach 73
    Death in Venice 73
Ashton, Roy **65**
Aspen 110
Aspen Award 110, 130
Astle, Ethel 3
Auden, Wystan 17, **18**, 18, 19, 21, 22, 23, 24, 25, 27, 30, 32, 33, 35, 36, 37, 38, 39, 40, 62, 69, 75, 76, 106, 127
    Composer, The 127; homosexuality 20; *Our Hunting Fathers* 19
Australia 115
Axel Johnson 40
Bach, Johann Sebastian 2, 15, 56, 57, 75, 116, 122
    St John Passion 116; *St. Matthew Passion* 15
Bakelite Plastics Ltd 52
Baker, Janet 119
Bali 94
Balinese music 95, 96
Balliol College, Oxford 25
Barbirolli, John 31
Barcelona 20
Barrie, J.M. 11
    Peter Pan 11
Barrutia, Andoni 23
Bartlett, Ethel 33
Basle 16, 52
Basle University 100
Bax, Arnold 11
Bayswater 9
BBC (British Broadcasting Corporation) 13, 41, 43, 103, 114, 116, 128
BBC Radio 3 118
BBC Singers 14, 22, 25
BBC Third Programme 62
Beaton, Cecil 106
Beaulieu, Lord Montagu of 106
Beaverbrook, Lord 106
Bedford, Steuart 118
Beecham, Sir Thomas 16
Beethoven, Ludwig van 2, 7, 10, 20, 57, 89, 122
    Fidelio 20

Belsen 59
Benjamin, Arthur 9, 16
Bentwaters 115
Berg, Alban 6, 14, 16, 18, 122
    Violin Concerto 18
Beriosova, Svetlana 96
Berkeley, Sir Lennox **19**, 19, 20, 21, 22, 23, 24, 25, 28, 43, 53, 81, 127
    Mont Juic 19
Berkeley, Michael 43
Berkshire Festival 62
Berlin 52, 57
Bernstein, Leonard 52, 62, 77
Biennale Festival 90
Bing, Rudolf 61
Birmingham Post, The 50
Blair, David 96
Blake, William 6, 78
    Songs of Innocence 78
Blom, Eric 50
Blyth, Alan 118
Blythburgh Church 114
Bolshoi Theatre 108
Bombay 94
Bonavia, Ferruccio 50, 61
Boosey & Hawkes 16, 27, 85, 110
Boston 114
Boston Symphony Orchestra 36, 79
Boult, Sir Adrian 41
Bradbury, Ernest 125
Brahms, Johannes 2, 8, 10, 55
Brannigan, Owen **98**
Bream, Julian 97, 110
Brecht, Bertolt 114
Brett, Philip 53, 128
Bridge, Ethel 10
Bridge, Frank **5**, 5f, 9, 10, 11, 19, 21, 23, 24, 26, 55
    Enter Spring 5; *Sea, The* 5
British Council 67, 113
British Library 128
British Music in our Time 58
British Music Week 116
Britten (nee Hockey), Edith Rhoda **1**, 1f, **2**, 5, 16, **20**, 20
Britten (Welford), Beth 2, **3**, 8, **11**, 11, 19, 20, 21, 23, 25, 28, 29, 47, 77, 121
Britten Festival 112
Britten, Barbara 1, **3**, **9**, 9, 20, 25, 74, **76**, 76, 121
Britten, Benjamin 1ff, **3**, **5**, **20**, **26**, **27**, **30**, **32**, **33**, **36**, **68**, **72**, **73**, **76**, **82**, **90**, **94**, **97**, **101**, **102**, **103**, **105**, **107**, **109**, **110**, **111**, **113**, **117**, **120**, **123**, **124**, **126**, **127**, **131**
    Albert Herring 53, 62, 64, 65f, 79, 97, 111, 129, 130; *American Overture, An* 39; *Ash Grove, The* 55; Aspen Award, receives 110; authors 88; *Bagatelle* 8; *Billy Budd* 79, 80, 81, 82, 83, 103, 112, 124; birth 1; *Birthday Hansel, A* 119; *Boy was Born, A* 14f, 21; *Burning Fiery Furnace, The* 112; Cambridge, receives honorary doctorate in music 100; *Canadian Carnival* 27, 31; *Cantata academica* 100, 130;

Cantata Misericordium 107; *Canticle 1 (My Beloved is Mine)* 56; *Canticle V (The Death of Saint Narcissus)* 118; cars 33, 88, 90; *Cello Sonata* 107; *Cello Symphony* 107, 109; *Ceremony of Carols, A* 40, 125, 129; *Chaos and Cosmos (Symphonic Poem in E)* 5; childhood 1ff; *Children's Crusade* 114, 124; Cobbett Prize 12; Companion of Honour, created 85; *Company of Heaven, The* 22; conscientious objection 41; Crag House (4 Crabbe Street) 67; *Curlew River* 96, 108, 109, 110, 111, 112; death 121ff; *Death in Venice* 53, 116ff, 123, 124, 129; *Diversions for piano and orchestra* 31; domestication 89; *Early one morning* 55; family home **2**; Farrar Composition Prize 11; fascism 18; *Festival Te Deum* 58; first concert with Pears 25; *First String Quartet* 33; flat (with Pears) 21; *Foggy Dew, The* 55; *Four Sea Interludes* 53; *Friday Afternoons* 15, 16, 129; funeral 121; *Gemini Variations* 109, 111; *Gloriana* 68, 72, 75, 83, 84, 85, 89, 96, 108; *Golden Vanity, The* 112; grave **123**; Hallam Street 25; heady boy 5; health 116ff; *Holiday Diary* 16; holidays 94; *Holy Sonnets of John Donne, The* 58, 74; homosexuality 20ff, 53; Hull University, receives honorary music doctorate 78; *Humoureske* 6; *Hymn to St Cecilia* 40; illnesses 8, 112, 116ff; last recital with Pears 117; leisure 88; *Les illuminations* 28, 31, 35, 96; *Let's make an Opera* 78; Life Peer (Baron Britten of Aldeburgh), created 85, 120; *Little Sweep, The* 78, 79, 94; Lowestoft, receives Freedom of Borough of 77, 87; *Mazurka elegiaca* 33; memorial stone (Westminster Abbey) 127; Mendelssohn Scholarship 12; *Midsummer Night's Dream, A* 100, 101, 102, 108, 116, 129; *Missa Brevis* 101; *Mont Juic* 19; *Nocturnal (for guitar)* 110; *Nocturne (for tenor and chamber orchestra)* 100; *Noye's Fludde* 70, 98, 99; *Occasional Overture* 62; Old Mill House, The **22**, 23, 24, 43, 47, 67; *On This Island* 22; Order of Merit, receives 85; *Our Hunting Fathers* 19 ; *Overture in B flat minor* 5; *Owen Wingrave* 53, 100, 114, 116, 130; Oxford University, receives honorary degree 108; pacifism 10, 18; painters 43f, 88; *Paul Bunyan* 32, 33, 35, 38, 62, 118, 120, 129; *Peter Grimes* 34, 36, 41, 44, 46ff, 57, 59, 61, 62, 66, 68, 70, 71, 79, 87, 107, 108, 113, 114, 128, 129; *Phaedra* 119; *Phantasy (for oboe quartet)* 14, 16; *Phantasy (for strings)* 12, 13; *Piano Concerto* 23, 24, 35; *Poet's Echo, The* 111; *Praise we great men* 121; *Prince of the Pagodas, The* 96, 97; *Prodigal Son, The* 112, 113; *Psalm 150* 11; *Quatre Chansons Français* 6; *Rape of Lucretia, The* 58, 59, 61, 62, 63, 64, 67, 111, 130; Red House, The **72**, 89, 97, 119, 120, 125, 126, 128; *Rejoice in the Lamb* 58; *River, The* 101; *Royal Failiy, The* 2; Royal Philharmonic Society Gold Medal, receives 111; *Sacred and Profane* 119; *Saint Nicolas* 68, 69, 93, 94, 126, 129; *Sally Gardens, The* 42, 55; *Scottish Ballad* 33; *Second String Quartet* 58, 131; *Serenade (for tenor, horn and strings)* 46, 100, 107; service of thanksgiving 126; *Seven Sonnets of Michelangelo* 32, 43, 44; *Simple Symphony (for strings)* 15; *Sinfonia da Requiem* 31, 35, 36, 40, 79, 96, 107; *Sinfonietta* 12, 16; *Six Hölderlin Fragments* 107; *Songs and Proverbs of William Blake* 111; *Songs from the Chinese* 97; *Spring Symphony* 73, 79, 129f; Story of Music, The (Wonderful World of Music, The) 99; *Suite for violin and piano* 16; *Suite on English Folk Tunes* 118; Sullivan Prize 12; *Symphony in D minor* 5; *There's none to soothe* 55; *Third String Quartet* 119, 121, 123; *Third Suite for Cello* 116; *Three Fugues for Piano* 10; *Three Two-part Songs* 12; *Trios in fantastic form* 5; *Turn of the Screw, The* 82, 90, 92, 93, 94, 97, 100, 111, 116, 129; USA visit 25ff; *Variations on a Theme of Frank Bridge* 21, 28, 29; *Violin Concerto* 27, 31; *Voices for Today* 111; *Waly, Waly* 55; *War Requiem* 70, 104, 109, 123, 126, 129; *Welcome Ode* 120, 129; *Who are these children?* 115; *Winter Words* 107, 122; *Young Apollo* 27, 62; *Young Person's Guide to the Orchestra, The* 62f, 96, 129

Britten, Benjamin: a Commentary on his work from a group of specialists 70, 75
Britten, Benjamin: His Life and Operas 71
Britten, Robert (Bobby) 1f, **3**, 11, 106
Britten, Robert Victor **1**, 5, 15
Britten-Pears Foundation 86
Britten-Pears Library 128
Britten-Pears School for Advanced Musical Studies 128
Brosa, Antonio 31
Buchenwald 59
Budapest 52, 109
Burra, Peter 19, 20, 21
Burrell, Billy 94
Caesar 4
Calcutta 94
Campsey Ash 64
Canadian Broadcasting Corporation 27
Caplan, Isador 120
Carpenter, Humphrey 40, 44, 76, 86, 90, 119, 122
    Benjamin Britten 122
Catskill Mountains 29
Cavalcanti, Alberto 16
Cecilia, Saint 1
Chapel House, Horham **115**, 115, 118, 119
Chapman, Joyce 8
Chelsea 10
Chopin, Frederic 8
Christ Church, Oxford 17
Christie, Audrey 61
Christie, John 59, 62, 66
Cincinnati Symphony Orchestra 33f
Cinderella 2
City Of Birmingham Symphony Orchestra 39
Clark, Sir (Lord) Kenneth 63, 81
Cleveland Orchestra 39
Coal Face 17
Coldstream, William 16
Coleman, Basil 81, 83, 92, 93, 97
Coleman, Charles 3
Collingwood, Lawrance 46
Columbia University 33
Composer and the Listener, The 16
Coolidge Quartet, The 33
Coolidge, Elizabeth Sprague 33, 34
Cooper, Martin 84, 124
Copenhagen 52
Copland, Aaron 25, **27**, 27, 29
Cosi fan tutte 45
Council for the Encouragement of Music and the Arts (CEMA) 42, 47
Covent Garden 79, 81, 85, 96, 103, 116, 118
Coventry Cathedral 104, **105**
Coward, Noël 121
    I'll see you again 121
Crabbe, George 34, 36, 47, 49, 57, 67, 68
    Borough, The 34; *Peter Grimes* 34, 36
Crag House (4 Crabbe Street) 67
Cranbrook, Countess of 67
Cranko, John 96, **101**, 102
Cross, Joan 46, 47, 48, **51**, 51, 59, 63, 64, **65**, 71, **84**, 83, 86, 91
Crown Film Unit 63
Crozier, Eric 7, 46, 47, **59**, 59, 60, 61, 62, 63, 64, 66, 67, 78, **79**, 80, 98, 105
Culshaw, John 125
Czechoslovakia 114
Daily Express, The 50
Daily Telegraph, The 12f, 44, 50, 124, 128

Darnton, Christian 12
Dartington Hall 64, 70
Davies, Meredith **105**
Dawson, Lynn **129**
Day-Lewis, Sean 128
de la Mare, Walter 12
Debussy, Claude 122
    Cello Sonata 122; *En blanc et noir* 122; *Nocturne* 122
Decca 110
Del Mar, Norman 77
Delhi 94
Delius, Frederick 11, 26
    Brigg Fair 11
Dilizhan (Armenia) 111
Disney, Walt 11
Donne, John 58
Douglas, Basil **90**, 92, 97
Dowland, John 110, 129
    Come, heavy sleep 110
Duncan, Roger 95
Duncan, Ronald 59, **60**, 60, 61, 64, 77, 95, 105
Dunkerley, Piers 23
Dyer, Olive **91**, 92
Eastbourne 10
Edinburgh 62
Edinburgh Festival 114
Elgar, Sir Edward 11, 14, 18, 54, 116, 126
    Dream of Gerontius, The 116; *First Symphony* 18; *Symphony No.2* 11
Eliot, T.S. 118
Elizabeth I, Queen 83
Elizabeth II, Queen 83, **113**, 113, 114, 119, 120, 121
Elmhirst, Dorothy 64, 70
Elmhirst, Leonard 64, 70
EMI 43
English Folk Song Society 55
English Opera Group 63, 67, 90, 92, 97, 111, 113, 115
Essex, Earl of 83
Evans, John 71
Evans, Nancy **60**, 60, 64, **66**, 67, 81
Evans, Peter 111
Evening News 50
Expo '67 113
Faber & Faber 110
Fass, Marjorie 18, 21, 23, 24
Ferrier, Kathleen **59**, 59f, 79
Festival of Britain 79
Fischer-Dieskau, Dietrich 104, **105**, 111
FitzGerald, Edward 68
Florence 14
Forster, E.M. 34, 68, 69, **79**, 80, 83, 88
Forster, Morgan 79
Framlingham Earl 5
Frankfurt 100
Freer, Dawson 46
Freud 2
Gamelan orchestra **95**
George VI, King 82
German, Edward 48
    Merrie England 48
Gielgud, Sir John 103
Gishford, Anthony 108
    Tribute to Benjamin Britten 108
Glasgow 62
Glock, William 42, 50
Glyndebourne 59, 60, 61, 62, 63, 64, 69
Glyndebourne English Opera Company 62

Goddard, Scott 58, 61
Golea, Antoine 92
Goodall, Reginald 48, 60
Goossens, Leon 14, 34
GPO (Post Office) 16
Graham, Colin 98f, 108, 109
Grainger, Percy 130
Gramophone 125
Grand Rapids 28
Graz 52
Greatorex, Walter 7, 8
Greenfield, Edward 118
Gresham The 8
Gresham's School, Holt **7**, 7f, 17
Grigson, Geoffrey 124
Griller Quartet 14
Guardian, The 118
Guthrie, Tyrone 46, 63
Halifax, Nova Scotia 40
Hamburg 52
Hardy, Thomas 89
    Winter Words 89
Harewood House 89
Harewood, Earl of 86
Harewood, Lord (George) **76**, 76, 81, 82, 84, 85, 94
Harewood, Marion 81, 82, 100
Harper, Heather 104, 114
Hawkes, Ralph **15**, 16, 25, 41, 63
Heinsheimer, Hans 27
Hely-Hutchinson, Victor 13
Hemmings, David **91**, 92
Henry VIII 105
Herbage, Julian 41
Hesse, Prince Ludwig of 94, 95, 97, 100, 111
Hesse, Princess Margaret of 94, 95, 97, 111
Heyworth, Peter 123
Hindley, Clifford 66
His Master's Voice 43
Holbrook 99
Hölderlin 100
Holland 73, 93
Holland Festival 66, 79
Holst, Gustav 5, 26, 42
    Planets, The 5
Holst, Imogen **42**, 42, 46, 49, 51, 61, 68, 70, 72, 75, 83, 89, 93, 95, 97, 99, 110, 113, 116
    Story of Music, The (Wonderful World of Music, The) 99
Hong Kong 96
Howes, Frank 56, 61, 81, 92, 102
Hudson, Nellie **89**, 89
Hullah, John 55
Humby, Betty 16
Hussey, Rev. Walter 58, 70, 75, 76, 126
Iken 64
India 111
Indonesia 94
International Red Cross 107
International Society for Contemporary Music, Festival of 14, 28
Ipswich, Bishop of 121
Ireland, John 9, 10, 11, 12, 53, 55, 82, 89, 93
Isherwood, Christopher **18**, 20, 22, 25
    homosexuality 20
James, Henry 90, 91, 106, 116
    Turn of the Screw, The 90, 116
Jeney, Gábor 109, **110**
Jeney, Zoltán 109, **110**
Johnson, Graham 75

Joyce, William (Lord Haw-Haw) 52
Jubilee Hall 67, 69, 79, **101**, 101, 121
Kallman, Chester 33
Karachi 94
Keller, Hans 45, 70, 75, 108, 128
Kennedy, Michael 44, 77, 97
Kennedy, President John 108
Kingsley 2, 78
  Water Babies, The 2, 78
Kodály, Zoltan 110
Koussevitzsky, Serge **36**, 36, 46, 62, 79
Kraft, Victor 29
Krips, Josef 86
Kubelik, Rafael 114
L'Express 92
La bohème 45
La traviata 45
Lambert, Constant 24
Lancing College 93
Lancing College Chapel **68**, 69
Leeds Town Hall 100
Leigh, Vivien 52
Leiston Modern School 99
Lenin 19
Leningrad (St Petersburg) 105, 109
Lewisohn Stadium 29
Listener, The 24, 34
Liverpool 41, 62
Lloyd Webber, Sir Andrew 129
London Boys Singers **124**
London Clinic 117
London Evening Standard 106
London Philharmonic Orchestra 19
Long Island 29
Los Angeles Times 34
Lovett, Martin 123
Lowestoft 2, 11, 18
Lucerne 67
Mackerras, Charles 98
Macnaghten, Anne 11
Macnaghten-Lemare Concerts 12
Magic Flute, The 45
Mahler, Gustav 10, 122, 123
Maine, Basil 21
Malcolm, George 101
Maltings, The 113, 114, 115, 117, 118, 128
  fire 114
Manchester 62
Manchester Guardian 84
Mandikian, Arda 91
Mann, Thomas 116, 117
  Death in Venice 116; *Tonio Kröger* 117
Mann, William 104
Mannheim 52
Marrakesh 112
Matthews, Colin 121
Maud, Jean 63, 66, 79, 90
Maud, John 63, 66, 79, 90
Maupassant 64
  Le Rosier de Madame Husson 64
Maxwell Davies, Sir Peter 129
  Kirkwall Shopping Songs 129
Mayer, Dr William 30, 46, 86
Mayer, Elizabeth 29, **30**, 32, 33, 34, 35, 36, 40, 41, 43, 76, 86
Mayer, Michael 30
Melksham 42
Melville, Herman 79f
  Billy Budd 79, 80

Mendelssohn, Felix 42
Menuhin, Yehudi 53, 58, **123**, 123
Michelangelo 44, 58
Milan 52
Miller, Charlie 35
Mitchell, Donald 1, 19, 56, 69, 70, 75, 96, 110, 114, 120, 128, 130
Mitchell, Kathleen 120
Montgomery, Field-Marshall 52
Montreal 27, 113
Moore, Henry 96
Moscow Conservatory 109
Mozart, Wolfgang Amadeus 75, 114, 116, 122
  Idomeneo 114; *Requiem* 116
Munich 16
Music Lover 12
Music Review 50
Musical Opinion 84
Musical Times 128
Mussolini 18
National Heart Hospital 117f
Neel, Boyd 21
Nehru, Pandit 94
Neville-Smith, Esther 93
  Friar's Acre 93
New English Singers 25
New Statesman 81
New Statesman and Nation 43
New York 27, 29, 52, 111, 113, 114
New York Festival 28
New York Metropolitan Opera 118
New York Philharmonic Orchestra 31
New York Public Library 39
New York Sun 31
New York Times 61, 78, 115
New Zealand 115
Newman, Ernest 50, 70, 84
News Chronicle 61
Nielsen, Flora **60**, 60
Nietzsche 117
Night Mail **17**, 17
Nolan, Sydney 116
North Lancing 93
Northcott, Bayan 123
Norway 120
Norwich Festival 5, 19
Notre Dame 20
Obey, André 59
  Le viol de Lucrèce 59
Observer 42, 50, 84, 123
Offenbach, Jacques
  Tales of Hoffmann, The 41
Old Mill House, The **22**, 23, 24, 43, 47, 67
Ontario 97
Opera 12, 125
Orford Church 98, **99**, 109, 112
Ormandy, Eugene 31
Osborne, Charles 69
Owen, Wilfred **104**, 104, 123
Oxford 62
Oxford Book of English Verse, The 9
Oxford University 108
Oxford University Press 12, 15
Palmer, Christopher 6
Palmer, Tony 128
  Time there was, A 128
Paris 16, 111
Parr, Gladys **65**

Peace of Britain 18

Pears, Sir Peter 7, 8, 19, 21, 24ff, **27**, **30**, **32**, **45**, **51**, **66**, **68**, **82**, **84**, **90**, **101**, **105**, **110**, **111**, **117**, **120**, **124**, **127**, **129**
    conscientious objection 41; *Così fan tutte* 45; first concert with Britten 25; flat (with Britten) 21; homosexuality 28ff; knighthood 127; *La bohème* 45; *La traviata* 45; Lancing College 69; last recital with Britten 117; London house 73, 86; *Magic Flute, The* 45; *Merrie England* 48; painting 88; parents 73; *Rigoletto* 45; sexuality 7; *Tales of Hoffmann* 41

Performing Right Society, The 125
Periton, Leslie 120
Philadelphia Orchestra 31
Phoenix Theatre 52
Piper, Clarissa **90**
Piper, Edward **90**
Piper, John 59, 63, 81, 83, **90**, 90, 96, 116
Piper, Myfanwy **90**, 90, 116, 116, 118
Plomer, William 68, 82, 83, 84, 85, 93, 96, 101, 108, 112
Poland 103
Potter, Mary **97**, 97
Poulenc, Francis 108
Pounder, John 32
Prague 109
Pravda 107
Promenade Concerts 23, 24, 108
Purcell, Henry 55, **56**, 56, 58, 63, 122, 129, 130
    Divine Hymns 56; *Fantasia upon one note* 130
Purdie, Claire 42
Pushkin 111, 112
Quebec 27
Queen Mother 126
Rachmaninov, Sergei 8
    Polichinelle 8
Racine 119
Radio Times 14
Rattle, Sir Simon 39
Ravel, Maurice 5, 6
    Shéhérazade 6; *String Quartet* 5
Ravenscroft, Thomas 19
Reeve, Basil 2
Reiss, Stephen 25, 116
Rice, Tim 129
Richter, Sviatoslav 122
Rigoletto 45
Rio de Janeiro 113
Ritchie, Margaret **45**,
Robertson, Rae 33
Rodzinski, Artur 39
Rostropovich, Mstislav **103**, 103, 105, 107, 108, **109**, 109, 111, 114, 116, 122
Rothman, Bobby **35**, 35
Rothman, David 31, **35**, 35, 36
Royal Albert Hall 118
Royal College of Music **9**, 9, 14
Royal Festival Hall 108
Royal Philharmonic Society 111
Sackville-West, Edward 54, 61
Sadler's Wells Opera Company 45, 46, 47, 108
Sadler's Wells Theatre 47, 50, 51, 59, 85, 93
Salzburg 16
Salzburg Mozarteum 21
Salzburg Volksblatt 22
Samuel, Harold 5
Sauerlander, Beata 6f, 29, 31
Scherchen, Hermann 24
Scherchen, Wolfgang (Wulff) **24**, 24, 25, 27, 32, 43

Schiøtz, Aksel **60**, 60
Schönberg, Arnold 8, 10, 95, 128
    Pierrot lunaire 8, 9; *Six Little Piano Pieces* 13
Schubert, Franz 55, 75, 76, 114, 126
    Die Winterreise 114; *String Quartet* 126; *Trout Quintet* 76
Schumann, Robert 42
Scotland Yard 106
Servaes, Bill 118, 119
Servaes, Pat 119
Shakespeare, William 59, 100, 102
Sharp, Cecil 55
Sharp, Frederick **66**
Sharp, Geoffrey 50
Shawe-Taylor, Desmond 81, 103, 105, 123
Shostakovich, Dmitri **103**, 103, 105, 112
    First Cello Concerto 103
Sibelius, Jean 125
    Sixth Symphony 125
Sicily 94
Singapore 94
Sitwell, Edith 93, 121
Slater, Enid 25, 27, 41
Slater, Montagu 41, 44, 64, 105
Smart, Christopher 58
Snape 21, 23, 47, 64, 67, 89, 113, 121
Solti, Sir George 103, 125
Sotheby's 52
Soutar, William 115
South Lodge School **4**, 4f
Southampton 26
Soviet Union 103, 107, 109, 111, 116
Spectator 84
Spender, Stephen 86
SS Ausonia 26
St. John's Church, Lowestoft 2
St. Matthews, Northampton 58
Stadlen, Peter 44
Stein, Erwin 82, 85, 97, 110
Stein, Marion 74, 86
Stock, Frederick 35
Stockholm 52
Strachey, Lytton 83
Strand Theatre 41
Stratford 97
Strauss 37
Strauss, Richard 74
    Alpine Symphony 74
Stravinsky, Igor 7, 10, 11, 61, 77, 105
    Firebird, The 8; *La sacre du printemps (The Rite Of Spring)* 10; *Oedipus rex* 61; *Symphonie de Psaumes* 11
Strode, Rosamund 110
Sullivan, Sir Arthur 54
Sumidagawa 96
Sunday Telegraph, The 123
Sunday Times, The 50, 70, 84, 92, 123
Sweden 93
Tait, Ian 117
Tanglewood 52, 62
Tchaikovsky, Peter Ilich 96, 122
Thant, U 111
Thomson, Rita **117**, 118, 119, 120, 121, 128
Thorpe, Jeremy 86
Time 33
Time & Tide 50
Times, The 13, 24, 43, 50, 56, 61, 66, 81, 84, 92, 102, 104, 118, 124
Tippett, Sir Michael **48**, 48, 53, 61, 82, 123
Tokyo 96, 103

Totnes 70
Ufford 64
United Nations 111
Uppman, Theodore 81
Vaughan Williams, Ralph 9, 10, 14, 19, 53, 54, 55, 56, 57, 84
    Fantasia on Christmas Carols 11; *Five Tudor Portraits* 19;
    Fourth Symphony 14
Venice 90, 93, 94, 102, 108, 113, 116, 119
Verdi, Giuseppe 108, 122
Vienna 14, 16, 85
Vienna Boys' Choir 112
Vishnevskaya, Galina **104**, 104, 114
Voltaire 84
Vyvyan, Jennifer **91**, 91
Waddington, Sidney 9
Wagner, Richard 6, 16, 37, 122, 128
    Die Meistersinger 16
Wales 118
Walton, William 11, 12, 13, 14, 53, 54, 55, 108
    Façade 11; *Viola Concerto* 11
Water Babies, The 3
Welford, Kit 38
Wentworth Hotel 68
Westminster Abbey 126, 127

Westminster Cathedral 101
Westminster, Dean of 126
White, Eric Walter 70, 72
Wigmore Hall 43, 44
Wilbye Consort 119
Wilde, Oscar 20
Wilder, Thornton 52
    Skin of our Teeth, The 52
Williamson, Malcolm 123
Wittgenstein, Paul 31
Wolf, Hugo 43
Wood, Sir Henry 23
Woodger, Cissie 64
Woodstock 29
Woolverstone Hall 99
Wordsworth, William 6, 100
Wright, Paul 12
Wyss, Sophie 19, 28, 31
Yerevan 112
Yorkshire Post 125
Yugoslavia 103
Zagreb 94
Zurich 52